I0818420

Alive Now

Alive Now

Un Dia a La Vez
(One Day at a Time)

Paul E. Daniels

Alive Now: One Day at a Time

Published by Clovercroft Publishing, Franklin, Tennessee

Published in association with Shane Crabtree of Clovercroft Publishing
www.clovercroftpublishing.com

Cover and Interior Design by Suzanne Lawing

ISBN: 978-1-968127-31-2 (print)

Printed in the United States of America

DEDICATION

First and foremost, I dedicate this book to my parents, Kevin and Leonor. They are the ones who gave me life, a heart for blood to run through my veins, air in my lungs, eyes to see, and a brain to use, which inspired me to write this book.

I also dedicate this book to my past, present, and future wife, "Lady" Kristen, who has been a part of my life for more than 23 years. She is my soulmate and has been the best supporter of my journey. I love you, and I'm extremely blessed that we get to spend this life together—Alive!—raising our Triple A batteries, Annelise, Adelynn, and Ava.

AUTHOR'S NOTE

As a Mexican-American who was born and raised in the United States, I write this book as my effort to provide experience, strength, and hope to those who live with mental illness and co-occurring disorders such as alcoholism and drug addiction.

This book is designed to be a memoir of some—but not all—of my life experiences, which have shaped who I am today.

There have been several heroes that I will recognize throughout the book, those who have contributed to our family still living today. I encourage the reader to relate to the stories as much as possible—thinking of your parallel stories while you do—as I have written them from my life's perspective.

My hope is the reader will relate to these actual events and understand that, no matter what happens in your life, you have decisions to make and choices to make that will shape the sail of your life journey. I understand that everybody on this planet has different trials and tribulations, but a common thread is with us all. The only constant in life is *change*.

I will start with some words of wisdom from one of my mentors, Alan Birchfield, mixed with my own: "Change is inevitable, but growth is optional." You are Alive NOW today, so begin there.

WHY I WROTE THIS BOOK

In February of 2021 I experienced a life threatening tragic event. I suffered a medical episode or what healthcare professionals would consider an acute manic episode. I was locked inside a cellblock in solitary confinement for seven nights naked wondering how I got myself here. Instead of filing a lawsuit against the hospital for medical malpractice, I have decided to write this book.

Hopefully those who suffer from mental illness and drug and alcohol addiction will see that recovery is a choice one can make just as easily and as often as harmful choices. The hard part is realizing that. Believe me, I know. My goal with this book is to talk openly and honestly and help others who have found themselves in spots similar to mine.

Together, I believe, we can help one another.

CONTENTS

ONE

Manic Episodes, an Isolation Cell, and . . . Hope

I am standing naked in a solitary confinement jail cell. It's deafeningly silent and so very cold. How did I get here? Did I die? Is this Hell? The moments before were so chaotic and hard to explain. It was like I was going in and out of a dream state, and I truly felt like I was so far away from my reality.

It is February 15, 2021, in the middle of a pandemic in the Bernalillo County Metropolitan Detention Center outside Albuquerque, New Mexico during a record-breaking snowstorm. I had no idea how long I had been away from my family, and I certainly didn't know how I ended up in this solitary confinement cell buck naked. It's been seven nights and I'm in solitary confinement. I'm naked, and I do not understand how

I came to be here. Am I in a dream? Am I going to live the rest of my life in this cell? Am I going to die here? How did I get here? And where is this going to lead?

Allow me to go back, so I can work forward . . .

Before this, I had gone on a ski trip with my friends, in late January 2021, to Jackson Hole, Wyoming. We were staying at a very nice ski-in/ski-out resort. I am there, really, just to have a good time. We had rented some snowmobiles. One of my friends, Chris, actually wrecked one, flipping it, on our second day.

It's the week before my birthday, and the world is going through a pandemic. I believe this ski trip triggered my episode. To explain that, I have to go back even further . . .

Seventeen years earlier, in 2004, I had been on a ski trip in Breckenridge, Colorado. Ski jumping with my friend Jasper, I suffered a traumatic brain injury. I had attempted a 25-foot jump at about 25 miles per hour but landed on my head. When Jasper got to me, I was foaming at the mouth, unconscious. I woke up in the hospital, quite literally unaware of how I got there.

I was 21 on that weekend, and a month later I'm going to a psychiatric care center to be treated for mental illness.

My doctor had told me the 2004 traumatic brain injury was the probable cause for my mental health illness diagnosis for bipolar disorder.

So the Jackson Hole trip was literally the 17-year anniversary of that accident that changed the course of my life forever. Now I need to introduce another possible factor: to this day, I am not sure if the triggering of 2004 was the leading effect of my 2021 episode, or if the Covid vaccine shot I had taken a week prior to the trip also had some effect, but, I will tell you, I was definitely in an acute manic episode during the Jackson Hole trip.

It has to be said that during this time in my recovery I had a medicinal marijuana card and used THC to help me with my anxiety and my sleep. It also helped to have something that I didn't think was as damaging as alcohol when socializing. I didn't have a drop of alcohol, but I did use THC in a few forms. Let's just say it was all a recipe for disaster masquerading as an amazing time with great friends enjoying ourselves in one of the most beautiful places on Earth. I used what I was able to purchase with my medicinal marijuana card under the pretense that I was helping myself, but in reality, I was not. Hindsight being 20-20, I just wanted to be—and still just want to be—happy and free.

Today, I've been living with bipolar disorder for twenty-two years, and I've been hospitalized for it three times, and I attended Cottonwood Rehabilitation Center on my own free will.

For someone who lives with bipolar, an acute manic episode is a severe form of mania. It is very much characterized by a distinct period of abnormally elevated, expansive, or irritable moods. It's described as an extremely unstable euphoric or irritable mood, often accompanied by excessive activity and energy levels, rapid thoughts and speech, reckless behavior, and even feelings of invincibility. For Bipolar One disorder patients, it can also come with increased goal-directed activity or energy. This period can be sustained for a week or longer, and sometimes hospitalization is necessary for a patient to be stabilized. Still other things that can accompany an episode are thoughts of grandiosity and a perceived decreased need for sleep.

In short, you feel as if you're on a high, but you're actually delirious and have delusions of self-importance.

Here are some examples of how I have lived through this.

There was a time in my life when I thought I was Jesus Christ and the most important person on the planet. There was a time when I was in an attic thinking that every helicopter and airplane was looking for me; I was in a manic episode of complete paranoia. There was a time I was driving 100 miles per hour in a 40 mph zone, running every red light, absolutely paranoid and terrified that people were after me. I thought every camera on the road was watching me. You hear voices in your head telling you, "Run away, run away."

I would go six or seven days with less than three hours of sleep each night.

In an acute manic episode, to explain the number of thoughts that run through your brain every day is one thing; to stop thinking and rest is nearly impossible. It's almost as though there are fifteen to twenty different voices in your head, each day, throughout the day, telling you constantly different things. It's one idea after the next idea after the next, and you're dealing with a constant overflow of emotions. As your mind races, you believe you can achieve every one of those ideas. Again, it's a state of euphoria, and you have delusions that you can conquer the world. You can feel as though you are very happy, but it's not real.

You forget to eat. You forget to sleep. You forget to drink fluids. You forget to be in the moment with your family, and if anything doesn't go your way, you act like a two-year-old and throw a temper tantrum and run away and get angry and scream and yell—and move on to the next place in your life to try to find what you're looking for. There was even a time in my life when I thought I was going to be the next governor of New Mexico.

So, during my episode in 2021, I was extremely agitated. My doctor recommended I take a different medication. Unfortunately, this medication had an adverse reaction, affecting my mental health. For about two weeks before I was hospitalized, my wife, dad, and children tried to stabilize me at our home in Corrales, New Mexico. I felt paranoid, restless, and discontent and had no idea what was wrong with me. My wife and parents refused to let me have the keys to my truck.

After about two weeks, I decided to take the spare keys—and I literally almost ran over my mom when I drove out of the driveway. In this acute state of mania, I was driving recklessly. My parents and wife called law enforcement and tried to tell me that I needed help . . .

This led to being detained in Albuquerque by about eight police officers who surrounded me in the downtown area and booked me into a hospital for mental health treatment.

* * * * *

So now I am in jail, but the last thing I remember from yesterday was being in the hospital—that I will not name—in psychiatric care being treated for the acute manic episode. It is all really a blur, and the thoughts are not clear. The Benzodiazapine that was being given to me at home had a paradoxical effect, and they were still giving it to me even though my wife was calling every chance she could, trying to reach someone to let them know that it was not working. I was able to call home to hear my wife's voice for a certain part of the day. Even my doctor who had been seeing me for fifteen years told them the same thing. Anyway, it is Valentine's Day, and I am trying so hard to escape the hospital to get to my wife and children on this holiday. Instead, I feel trapped inside this medical building. I am constantly roaming the halls, either barefoot or with only socks on, all day long, twenty hours a day, talking to the other mental health care patients.

So much of this information is not from my memory, but mostly the medical report that was released to me along with the police report.

The hospital has reached a point in which they have to tie me to a table and use hospital security to inject me in my right arm with a type of tranquilizing medicine. Following a medical blackout from a severe reaction to the injection, I proceed to shove my knee into a doctor's head, and this leads to him going to the hospital emergency room in a coma.

Later, I cold-cock a nurse with a closed fist.

Valentine's Day was always a holiday near and dear to my wife and children. Our usual tradition was for me to cook either a spaghetti dish or steak and potatoes with salad. We also shared Valentine's Day cards, flowers, gifts, chocolates, and memories as we loved one another as a family. I knew that being hospitalized during Valentine's Day was a lonely time for my family without me at home. So, being in a mental institute in Albuquerque, on Valentine's Day, I only have the thought that I should escape and get back home.

This led to assaulting the doctor, then the nurse.

I also would like to disclose the fact that in the medical report it said that the staff member on call went into the room that housed the medicines that they would need to administer their patients. It says that they were looking for one drug, but they couldn't find it, opened another, and then ended up finding the first drug they had been looking for and giving it to me intravenously.

The Albuquerque Police Department is dispatched at 4 AM. When they arrive they have to taze me three times to finally get me calm. (Later, I am told that if I had died in this hospital it would have been a justifiable death since I was completely out of control and out of mind.)

I am booked into jail and charged with two felony counts of battery against a health care worker.

Next, I am booked in a solidarity confinement jail cell for seven nights. Being in solitary confinement is an extremely trapped place, and feeling. Unfortunately, the emotions, mentally, are almost equal to how you are trapped physically. There is only the feeling of wanting to be free and outside of that cell.

I literally think I am going to die in this cell, or at least spend the rest of my living days—for however long—here. All the walls are made of cinder block and painted white. There is a toilet and a sink and a light that remains on twenty-four hours a day. The room is about 10 feet by 12 feet. There is a green mattress pad on the floor with a blanket, no pillow, and a glass window of about 12 inches by 12 inches. Last, there is a drop box so guards can deliver bologna sandwiches and cereal bars for some amount of nutrition. Twice a day a nurse will enter to administer medication and tell me to go to sleep. I don't think I ever truly sleep in this cell; the lights are always on and I am naked. Again, one of my few thoughts is that I will die in this wretched place.

* * * * *

In the meantime, my wife Kristen and parents were desperately fighting for me the entire week I was in that cell. Due to it being Covid-restricted time in the state of New Mexico, everything was done via Zoom. They hired an attorney and went to several courts seeking to allow my release. After my wife and parents convinced the judge I was mentally ill, the court determined that I would be released to the University of New Mexico Hospital Psychiatric Care Center for yet another week in a mental health institute, but that one actually cared. My father would eventually take custodial care of my well-being and, once stable, I would be under house arrest for thirty days at my parents' house.

Since I was facing two felony counts of assault, I had to prove to the courts that this was a response to being given the wrong medication for my mental illness and not my usual behavior.

In order to get a better understanding of what happened, I believe the reader should have more information about my family history and the background of who I am. In my case, my roots brought me a desire for success, and I was always encouraged to follow my dreams no matter how big and bold they seemed. Our foundations matter a lot. I hope it resonates with you.

This is my story, and today I am grateful to be alive now.

TWO

Background and Family History

Mom

Imagine being 18 years old and your mother has just died from ovarian cancer. You're one of eleven children. You're living in Chihuahua, Mexico, and your dream is to go to the United States to live a better life in the land of opportunity. One morning you wake up and decide: *I'm going to leave my home, my father, my younger siblings, and everything and everyone I've lived my whole life with.*

So, step back to 1976. Leonor and brother Henry are on a mission to go to the Rio Grande River and cross the border to find older siblings already living in Bloomfield, New Mexico. The only thing they take is the clothes on their backs and hopes and dreams that they will live a better life. No food, no money, no job, no knowledge of the English language—just hopes and dreams of a better life.

This dream became a reality to my mother, Leonor, and now it's part of my story. She is one of the heroes of my life, and I wouldn't be here without her. Today I feel a deep sense of gratitude for her bravery. Thank you for crossing the Rio Grande, Mama, and coming to the Land of Enchantment.

Dad

Imagine being 18 and you're one of eight children. Once again, it is 1976. Your father decides to move his family from Wilmington, Delaware to Bloomfield, New Mexico. You have just graduated from high school and will be moving to a place where, honestly, you have no idea what work you can get or what you can do. Your father, who is an electrical engineer, has just taken a job to work on a massive electrical power plant in the Animas Valley of New Mexico. Your mom and siblings have no idea what they're getting into, but they decide to pursue this opportunity, as a family.

Thank you, Dad, for moving to Bloomfield, New Mexico.

* * * * * * *

This is how my parents came to the same small town in New Mexico. They would cross paths in a restaurant named Roadside Inn, in Bloomfield, where my mother was a cook and my father a Bloomfield police officer. Like a lot of young kids at that time, dating was simple, involving simple pleasures. They remember an early date, at a drive-in theater, seeing the classic type of comedy that only Cheech & Chong could do, *Up in Smoke*. My dad was thinking there might be some Spanish in the movie as well. They dated about three years, married in the summer of 1981 in Bloomfield, then went to Las Vegas and Disneyland (California) for their honeymoon.

My father would later join the New Mexico State Police Academy where he graduated first in his class and was later stationed in the little town of Espanola. This was a solid several-hour drive east of Bloomfield, in the north-central part of the state. But after four years of turmoil from losing several friends and colleagues in the line of duty, living in a trailer in an elementary school yard, and rescuing inmates from one of the deadliest prison riots in American history—what are often called the Santa Fe Prison Riots—my mom reached a point where she decided going on as she had been was just not going to happen.

She gave my dad an ultimatum: "You either change jobs or change wives, because I can't put up with this anymore."

In 1981, my dad also lost his father in a tragic motorcycle accident. It was then that Dad's mom, my nanny, decided to move back to Wilmington, Delaware. This triggered my dad making a similar move.

With the ultimatum from my mom still ringing in his ears, my dad got serious and decided to move his family across the country to Wilmington, Delaware as well. He would soon take a job working at Silverbrook Memorial Park, a little cemetery where his father was laid to rest, and a cemetery he was familiar with. He had painted the fence of this cemetery when he was just a teen (15). My mom, who spoke very little English, if any, was in uncharted territory, living with her mother-in-law. Once again, she had left her wider family, now to start one of her own, two thousand miles to the north-east of her siblings.

* * * * *

I was born on a Friday in the winter of 1983; there was a huge blizzard in Wilmington. My Aunt Connie had two sons, Cesar and Antonio Jr. These two cousins are like brothers to me; they were in the hospital, along with my aunt Connie, the day I was brought into the world.

By that time, my uncle Antonio was gone. He was killed in an auto accident that left Connie alone to raise 5- and 3-year-old sons. Connie worked hard as a cook in a restaurant and, like my mom, a homemaker at home.

When my mom brought me into the world, she really had no one to be there with her. Connie and her two young sons showed up that day to support her, and that meant the world to my mom. Cesar and Antonio were just 9 and 8 at that time; they are just 13 months apart.

Connie's family didn't live anywhere near us, but every summer we seemed to find ourselves in the same town and spending lots of time together. They always seemed to "be around." This demonstrates how I began to think of them just like my brothers.

My aunt and her sons showed me that family is the most important thing in your life.

These were my first heroes—and they remain heroes to me to this day.

THREE

Childhood

In the fall/early winter of 1984-1985, my father interviewed with a large cemetery and funeral home company named Gibraltar Mausoleum. During the interview they asked him if he knew how to speak Spanish. My dad would proceed to say something in Spanish. The two brothers interviewing him said, "Sounds like Spanish to me" and "we have a job for you—in Corpus Christi, Texas. We would like for you to start Tuesday, January 2nd." My mother, who was nine months pregnant with my sister, Jessica, was preparing herself for another change in her life. So my parents, who have a two-year-old son, were preparing to move to Texas at the first of the year at the same time my mom was ready to deliver any day.

My dad let his new company know that his wife was due any day, and he would get there as soon as his little girl was born. After waiting almost three weeks after the due date, my father had to report to work in Corpus Christi no later than January 15 or the job opportunity would be lost. Dad decided to fly out so he could report to work on January 15, so my Aunt Connie and cousins Cesar and Tony Jr. once again were there for my mom at her delivery, which took place on January 15. Thus, due to sheer fate, my dad missed his baby girl's delivery by only a few hours.

My parents were once again uprooting for an incredible journey, raising two Mexican-American children in one of the most racially discriminating cities—for those of Mexican heritage—in the United States. My mom moved with her two very small children to Corpus Christi a week after Jessica's birth.

My dad had a full-time job, but my mother decided she needed to take a job as a cook at a restaurant named Kinko's, in Corpus Christi, to supplement the family income. There was a struggle, my parents told me, just to put food on the table. Still, that same year, 1985, they managed to sign the loan documents needed to purchase their first house.

In the spring of 1988 I come home from preschool and was asked about my school day. As a five-year-old, I proceeded to say, "I hate Mexicans." Honestly, my parents really hadn't dealt with much racial discrimination before this point. My mom was in tears; it became clear this would be a new reality. Racial discrimination, from this point on, was real and would impact my family's future.

One Sunday afternoon my father headed out to cut the grass. He had had a long week working at the cemetery. He gathered up the extra grass clippings in several garbage bags and left them on the curb for the trash men to pick up Monday morning. It's the end of a normal weekend, and he has work in the morning. Monday morning, my dad went out to his car to find someone had broken all the car windows, opened all the bags of grass clippings, and dumped them in his car. On the windshield of the car was a message: "We Hate Spics."

This was so traumatic for my parents that my dad felt like he needed to leave his job—which he was doing well at, and at which he was respected by all his peers, and respected them—and look to move. Fortunately, there was a lucky break for our family. When the owners of the company heard what happened and that my father wanted to leave Corpus Christi, they were taken back. He had been doing a great job over the last three years, and they knew he was worth keeping. Since the company also had funeral homes and cemeteries across Florida, they decided to transfer my father, and our family, to Tampa. This was the summer of 1988.

Our family moved so suddenly that my parents decided the best bet was to rent a house in Bradenton; my father would commute to work at least an hour every day. This move set me back a bit, so it took me two years to finish kindergarten. In the fall of 1990 I was set to start attending Pinehurst Elementary School. George Bush was the US president and the Gulf War in Kuwait—also known as "Desert Storm"—was in progress. I mention this because I distinctly remember American patriotism being rampant during this time. This was when Lee Greenwood's famous song "God Bless the USA" became such a hit (the first time around). It was so beautiful and, in my opinion, the most patriotic song in US history. In school, I learned the Pledge of Allegiance. I was a little guy, but I felt very proud to be an American.

Our family decided it was time to move once again, so we did, on what I remember was Halloween, October 31, 1990. We moved into a new development community in Valrico, Florida named River Hills, and this is where I would enjoy the best childhood, as I saw it, that any kid in the world could dream of.

First, there was a lot less discrimination. Even for a little guy, life just seemed very pleasant. Mom, once again to make ends meet, took multiple jobs at a florist and in retail. We had all we needed. It's these kinds of sacrifices that, as a child, you don't see, and you don't fully understand them for many years.

In 1991 there was a family that moved to our street from Mexico City. They had a little boy named Pablo who was about 7, and he loved to ride his bike on our street. One day he stopped by the house and noticed that my mom was from Mexico.

He would go back to his parents and his aunt and uncle, Nemesio and Sara Luisa, and tell them that there was a Mexican living on the same street, and that this family had two kids the same age as his siblings.

The Garcia Naranjo family and Gomez Obregon family would become part of our extended family for decades. They will be mentioned throughout this book.

Our family lived in Tampa from 1990 to 1996, and we enjoyed it, as these were pleasant years. I was quite the athlete, playing just about every sport, but my main sports were golf and basketball. My childhood friends were Kevin and Kyle, and we were fortunate that most days we could ride our bikes to school.

During those seven years in Tampa, Mom was always working one of her jobs. In the spring of 1996, my parents decided to purchase a lot so they could build a new house in the same neighborhood. But about three months later, bad news: the company my father was working for announced it would be selling the business. This one event changed the course of our family and our sweet life in Tampa. After the sale of the business, new management would come in and replace several positions, including my father's. My dad would interview with another company later that summer and eventually take a job . . . back in Texas, this time in Houston.

Once again, my parents decided to pack up and leave. In 1996, I was about to move to my fourth city in just 13 years of life. I know, compared to some, like military children, that may not be that many, but it was a lot of packing up and moving from my and my family's perspective.

My sister and I would be starting middle school in a new environment; we didn't know a soul on the new school campus the first day of school. I clearly remember how uncomfortable it was to walk through a large campus filled with faces I wasn't familiar with. In fact, I knew *no one.* Fortunately, once I made the basketball team, I was off and running with new friends.

Those were decent enough years, but change would once again take place in my life. In the summer of 1998 I was invited to continue my education in Mexico City at a school called Colegio Green Hills. I lived with Nemesio and Sara Luisa, and Pablo—that little boy riding his bike on my street in Tampa—would be my roommate for the school year. One of the most incredible parts of this opportunity was to be in the same class as the son of the President of Mexico, Ernesto Zedillo. Despite this being the fifth city I had lived in, I considered this opportunity amazing, to live in one of the largest cities in the world (a population greater than 20 million). I had the privilege of learning, in an in-depth way, about my Mexican culture, reading and writing in another language, and the history of such a beautiful country.

But there was a downside as well. During that brief time I would be introduced to nightclubs and alcohol—at the age of fifteen.

I have to be honest and tell you that I knew, even during those early years, that I was going to have a drinking problem. I found myself loving the taste and effects of alcohol. Alcoholism was on both sides of my family. But I also learned that I would be a black-out drinker from day one.

Despite living with this growing condition, I have to repeat: it was an incredible experience to live in Mexico City.

* * * * *

Before we moved from the Tampa area I actually had in my mind that I would be a professional golfer. I was being recruited by high school coaches and playing at a high level. But I sort of peaked, never really got any better, and moving so much probably hindered my development as well. The move to Mexico City—and getting a driver's license—almost certainly caused me to lose focus as well.

Though it was impactful on my life, I only spent seven months in Mexico City, and then I returned to Houston, in 1999, where I decided to get after the game of golf again. I joined the golf team at The Woodlands

High School. But in my head, very early on, I was telling myself that my social life was more important than playing golf, and that—or so I thought—drinking alcohol was the better choice.

I thought it was more important to get a part-time job and work selling shoes (my first job was at a Finish Line, for about a year) to pay for the booze that I was beginning to crave. I would soon learn this trick: if you could purchase a keg of beer for eighty dollars, all you would need to do is sell sixteen solo cups at five dollars each to pay for all the beer, and then you could pocket whatever you made after that.

Again, it became obvious I wasn't dedicated enough to golf. After three years of playing on the school team I decided to leave the team before my senior year. Even while I had this growing relationship with alcohol, I made this decision: in the fall of 2001 I took a part-time job at the local YMCA to work Monday through Friday from 3 PM to 7 PM after school. This was my senior year in high school, and instead of really going for it with golf or other things, I was thinking about helping others. I was an after-school counselor for younger kids.

This was also the place where I would, for the first time, meet my future wife.

Me and a best buddy, Frank, counseled 9- and 10-year-old boys at Glenloch Elementary School, helping them learn skills like archery, pool, other sports, and arts and crafts, and we would take them on field trips as well. We took care of details right down to making sure they got good snacks. Then we had to make sure their parents picked them up and signed them out by 7 PM. All in all, it was the perfect job for me, and the hours fit my schedule. There are more exciting things a high school senior could choose to do with his weekday afternoons after school, but I did enjoy the work. I do think it shows that, at heart, I care for people and had fun taking care of these kids.

I graduated from The Woodlands High School in May 2002. Now my transition into adulthood began. I would choose to enter the University of New Mexico (Albuquerque) in the fall of 2002.

FOUR

"My Lady": Kristen

I never thought the decision to work at the YMCA would lead to finding the love of my life, soul mate, and future wife, but it did. When we first met I was very attracted to Kristen, who, in time, I would grow to call, affectionately, "my lady." We would work together for about six months until we officially started dating in March 2002. I was reluctant to start dating since I would be graduating high school in less than two months, but we did, and I'm grateful for that decision.

I think she could see I really loved kids, and that was, sort of, the first thing she was attracted to. The year we met she was actually in her freshman year of college, at a community college, and she would soon go on to Texas A&M University.

Back at home my father had taken a job in New Mexico, and my mom was working for Continental Airlines. My sister was a junior in high school. I had been accepted to attend the University of New Mexico and planned on attending that fall. Kristen had been accepted to Texas A&M, and she would move to College Station in the summer of 2002, about the same time I would move to Albuquerque. Thanks to my mom's job at Continental, I would frequently fly back to Texas to visit Kristen. We would continue this long-distance relationship, dating throughout our college careers.

After graduating from Texas A&M in May 2006, Kristen accepted a job as a fourth-grade elementary school teacher at Colinas Del Norte in Rio Rancho, New Mexico. Our relationship grew much stronger when she decided to move to New Mexico. In the summer of 2006 Kristen rented an apartment and was set to start elementary school teaching that fall; I was entering my senior year in college. That summer, we decided to move in together; we were absolutely in love.

Kristen is one of the main heroes of my life as she took a huge risk with me in moving to New Mexico.

I struggled with addiction in my youth, and in these college years, and yet Kristen always believed in me and supported me; she displayed an incredible amount of love and backing. I often say that, in some ways, Kristen loves me more than I love myself.

I was working part-time at a funeral home and cemetery along with taking three summer classes at the University of New Mexico. With only three classes left to take in the fall of 2006 to graduate UNM, I would go to class, study, work at the funeral home and cemetery, get my life insurance license, and move into Kristen's apartment.

And also . . . drink. Whenever time permitted.

Kristen would talk to me about the times when I drank too much. I could detect her mood changing, but I wouldn't say too much directly. She showed great patience and love and kindness during the times I drank or used too much. I always hid just how much I self-medicated, but she always seems to know when things are off.

In many ways, I was oblivious, in denial of my drinking and using. I will be honest with the painful truth that I was unfaithful to her in dating, and even some after marriage. She seemed to have feelings when things were off and most times I would deny it. Often, this would happen during blackouts or heavy periods of drinking. In 2012 the infidelity stopped entirely. Kristen knew about all of this after the fact, and we are still in therapy. We work at our marriage, but sometimes I don't know if I can ever heal what I have hurt. It doesn't stop me from trying, and it is one of the reasons I live one day at a time.

However, all that is my perspective. For this book, Kristen sat down with my editor. Learning to love me, marrying me, and sticking with me has not always been easy. My editor interviewed her and she has contributed her own written account along with some of the interview. Here is Kristen's viewpoint on our relationship.

* * * * *

Kristen

As the wife of a person who struggles with mental illness and addiction, I tell Paul all the time that whether he likes it or not, his life with bipolar is intertwined with mine, not separate. Yes, we are on our own journeys in many ways, but his choices on whether he chooses detachment or working on himself affects me. I met him before his diagnosis when we were 19 and 20. I am four months older than him (he reminds me and everyone else as much as he can), and I graduated high school a year before he did. I stayed in town to attend community college to save on tuition costs and work part time. In writing this, I have to preface all of this with the fact that this has not been linear getting to this point in life. I have had to deal with many ups and downs within myself and with Paul as my partner in life. To be honest most of them are still being "dealt" with to this day. I have asked myself and him if being together was best for both of us so many times, but I am always brought back to my love for him and my vows that we have now said three times.

When we first met, I felt Paul was actually a little shy. I felt he was sweet, and very respectful, and we had a lot of mutual friends. And actually, my best friend was dating his best friend, so we were four little college kids, or almost into college, doing life, just jumping from party to party. One thing I always loved about Paul was that he always knew where the party was! He was quiet and reserved, but knew how to organize a good time.

He was also very responsible, always dressed nicely, and took charge to make me feel comfortable and special every time we were together. I also quickly found out he was patient and good with kids. We worked at an after school child care program together. The kids in our care were always so excited to see him. That said a lot to me. We knew he would be moving to New Mexico soon, but we got close fast and decided to keep in touch in college.

We didn't put too much pressure on each other because we knew we were young and we would find our way back to each other if it was meant to be. And we always did seem to find our way back to each other.

So when he was going off to New Mexico, and I was at Texas A&M, we were both kind of leaving our current realities. Our relationship became fluid and "on-again, off-again," but one thing remained; we had very similar mindsets in life. We both wanted a career and a family. At the same time, we were both in college; we knew this is when we were supposed to have fun and experience life. We just couldn't imagine life completely without each other. I think we still have that recurring theme to this day. After reading his words on this part of our life, I was shocked at how much he thought the drinking was out of control. I felt like it was typical for our age group and peers. We had fun, but we always reeled in the fun, studied, and worked hard to pass our classes and achieve our goals.

The drinking started to get scary for me when we went to college and drugs were introduced to Paul. Drugs were not our thing when we were in high school. Drugs were not part of my scene either. It was definitely around, but not something I was into. I feel like that is when the drinking got out of hand. There were times I wouldn't hear from him until the morning, and he would have stories of not remembering the night before, but he remembered he was driving with one eye open or he woke up laying on the side of the road. I remember being nervous for him and questioning why I was staying with him. I also remember feeling like "a paranoid girlfriend that needed to be put in my place" by people in his circle, and maybe someday I can elaborate on that, but I will keep it to myself for now. I guess I didn't want to leave him alone in what clearly was a struggle for him. I was always grateful when he visited, invited me to visit, or asked me to accompany him at a formal for his fraternity. We did this for five years.

Paul had the ski accident and was diagnosed with bipolar disorder in 2004. I never saw anything like that coming, but now that I look back, I see the entrance of a mental illness that has shaped our lives. It has shaped our lives like a violent volcanic eruption at times, but I have learned so much about myself, humanity, my spirituality, and my capacity for growth and my ability to love and be loved.

We were in two different states, so leading up to the diagnosis, my interactions with Paul were spotty, but from what his sister and friends were telling me, I knew things weren't right. I tried to piece together all of the information I was getting and even scheduled time to talk to my psychology professor about what was going on. I explained his accident, how he was juggling classes, student government, working at the family funeral business, and self-medicating the mental and physical pain from his injuries. I distinctly remember her telling me we would get him back, and everything that he was going through was indicative of bipolar disorder like I thought, but we could not diagnose him, of course. His doctor was the only one who could do that. She was so helpful, and I went out to visit him after his hospital stay.

After his diagnosis, he was able to get stable with medication and an amazing therapist. All of this was a huge blow to his identity. He was down for a long time, but we were so lucky the meds worked, and we were able to see each other because his mom worked for Continental Airlines and he was able to fly to see me in Texas. I saw him more than some of my roommates saw their boyfriends in other Texas cities.We grew closer and even more in love. I guess we felt like it was us against the world.

I think after coming to terms with the diagnosis myself and seeing how devastating it was for him and his family, it broke my heart. As an education major I learned so much about mental illness, and I saw the importance of awareness and inclusion and wanted to learn more about this illness that my boyfriend was now living with.

Obviously, I was young and naively optimistic. I have been accused of having a Pollyanna outlook at times and I can agree, but it never entered my mind to say, "Well, this is too much, you are too much…goodbye." We carried out life knowing things were different, but looking back now, I wished we would have learned more then. Maybe we could have avoided some of the things we had to go through.

Paul was also super responsible in college before and after the ski accident and diagnosis. He would party at his fraternity house, but he would also get up in the morning with a suit and tie on to go to work. Paul was a student senator, an elected position in the student government at his university. He was also the treasurer for the fraternity house. He was trying to make a name for himself. We would even go to galas, and he would do philanthropic work, and he always looked up to his dad and the family business. He was enamored and so very passionate about this area of his life, so much so, that it has been a huge blow in times of depression.

As I mentioned before, his mom worked for Continental Airlines, so not only were we able to visit each other, we traveled. We went to Australia to visit his sister, to Beijing, and to Spain, later, where he proposed to me. And it felt like it was us against the world again. Bipolar disorder seemed like something in the back of our minds, but it didn't seem to hold us back. To my knowledge he wasn't using drugs and his drinking was not obsessive. For my twenty-third birthday, he told me to pick any city in the United States and we would take a trip there. I picked New York. I had him running all over that city and we even got to see *Rent* on Broadway. For a young girl from Southeast Texas and Houston suburbs who had never flown in her life, this was amazing. We loved exploring new cities together. We really just loved each other. We both finished college and started thinking about the future.

* * * * *

I mentioned before that in New Mexico, Paul started to dabble in other drugs, and that was never part of our scene in Texas when we were together. New Mexico seemed to open doors to cocaine, pills, and a lot of THC. That was not something I was ever interested in, and I noticed a considerable change in the pace of partying once that started. He did move out of the frat house, but he got an apartment with friends that shared his affinity for drugs. Once I moved there, there were some really hard days because I left everything to be with him, and his partying with the boys was still going on. I would go out with them, but I never saw drug use. To this day, I am so confused how I never saw it happening, and it turned out it was all around me. Maybe I was too drunk to notice. I drank to keep up, but it got old fast for me. Somehow I thought by moving there, it would slow down. I guess it did, but not as much as I'd hoped.

I was a young fourth-grade teacher trying to find my way in a new state and what seemed to be a new world! After some hard conversations and boundaries I set up for myself, he seemed to put me first more and asked me to marry him when we were visiting his sister in Spain during spring break. I had no idea a proposal was coming. I was under the mindset that I promised myself, and him, I would give it a year and see where we were. At the same time I was so happy he did ask me, and it was so dreamy and thoughtful the way he did it.

We decided to have a year-long engagement. There was a lot of time for me to find out more about myself working as a teacher and living in beautiful New Mexico. When you have no friends and family around you, I think it becomes clear that you have to find out who you are. I also fell in love with the Sandia Mountain that would greet me each day and help me find my way when I got lost. If you have ever been to Albuquerque, you know what I mean. If you are facing the mountain you are due East. I met a few friends in particular who became sisters to me and they still are to this day. They reminded me of my worth when I didn't see it in myself. As the mother to daughters who are teenagers and a preteen, I am preaching this so hard right now. Paul and I have made it our mission to help them choose healthy ways to deal with stress and healthy ways to deal with peer pressures surrounding drugs, alcohol, and unhealthy relationships.

I think as we got closer to the wedding date, Paul seemed to question who he was, what bipolar disorder was, and whether he even needed his medication.

With a bachelor celebration that was held in Mexico, late nights, drinking, and probably other drugs, mania was springing up on us again.

* * * * *

Right before we got married, during that bachelor weekend in Mexico, Paul experienced full-fledged mania, and we almost called off the wedding. It was supposed to be the most exciting time of our lives planning the wedding, and we had been doing it for almost a year. I felt like I was fighting to keep it all together. Our parents and we had already spent so much money; we were both so excited, and now we had mania. So many things were said to me by his parents and sister; deep emotions were felt. It definitely shaped who I am today. Today I can say that I learned to lean into what I thought was their perspective. I know they were going through so much pain, but trying to understand how they were feeling helped me get through my own pain—and sometimes even forget it existed. Part of me felt like we should cancel, but we were regularly seeing therapists, attending church and addiction groups, and his medication and mood was improving. It would have been one of the saddest blows to him if we called it off.

We got through the planning of the wedding and the ceremony, and Paul was stable, but still not 100 percent, as I saw things. We called off our honeymoon in Jamaica and celebrated in South Padre Island, Texas. Paul told me he was not going to drink anymore, and I was okay with that. We knew the commitment, wanted to start a family, and even had the dream of having kids some day—that was important to us. We were both very driven and worked hard at upholding our vows. The bipolar brain and the addicted brain that sometimes work simultaneously are so very cunning and so good at lying. I just never could walk away. I always came back to the fact that there was a lot of love and it wasn't his fault he had to live with this illness.

It seems like in the early days of our marriage I just always had faith in our vows. I still do. Bipolar disorder has an ugly way of making you question every emotion you give and every emotion you receive. "Is it real? Is it mania? Is it fear of life-gripping anxiety or depression?

Is it psychosis?" Was it me just being in "fix it mode" and working through trauma? Maybe. At times I still don't know for certain. But I always remembered the way Paul made me feel in the moments of clarity that made up the most time of our life together. Times of crisis break people, as they should sometimes. Sometimes letting go is the very best thing you can do, but somehow we grew through all of it even if it felt like we were crawling through it one day at a time. He was always willing to put in the work to help himself. We are still learning and growing.

Many of our hardest times with bipolar in our experience were brought on by recreational drinking and drug use coupled with high stress. We always called each mania a perfect storm with many components—and we still look at it this way to this day. It is just glaringly obvious that drinking and drug use were always the straw that broke the camel's back.

So as things went on with Paul, I took on the role of: *Well, he has this diagnosis, and I need to be there for him.* Really, it was just a mission written on my heart.

I have read every book I could get my hands on to understand Paul's illness and have some on my shelf right now waiting to be read. Paul has always been a very passionate guy, so when his mood became more stable, he would then go into a dark hole of shame and sadness. His parents and sister dealt with that too. I had to make it clear to his mom that I was on her side so many times during that first hospitalization—and even into the second one years later. I still feel like I have to prove my competency to the other lives that are affected by this journey. I think that also shows how loved Paul is. I am sure that it is mostly my own desire to learn to live with this and in turn I see my own flaws.

I don't want to just survive, I want to thrive with this illness; maybe not every day, but a majority of them. I would be reminded so many times by them that I will never know what it is like to be his mom or his sister. I may not know, but I sure have compassion for it. I have felt shame for not doing enough or the right thing in others' eyes, but I knew and still know it is Paul we were fighting for, and an illness couldn't stop what we had started. I can honestly say to this day I would do it all over again if I had to. I'd do things differently. I'd be louder about my truths. That is what keeps me standing to this day.

Hospitalizations in psychiatric units, to me, meant Paul was cut off from me completely so that he could get stabilized. During his last hospitalization, which resulted in his arrest, I was calling every shift change to let the charge nurse or anyone who would answer my call know who I was, who Paul was, and that he had three daughters who loved and missed him—and what meds hadn't been working for us. (At the first hospitalization we were not married, so I had zero input and very little information about it. I think that is why I was so immersed in my psychology class at the time.)

When he was out of UNMH I got to go and be with him. I just focused on creating peace and calm. I always wanted him to know he could count on me to be there for him.

Needless to say, it is in our "Wellness Recovery Action Plan" (WRAP plan) that a hospital stay is a last resort option, and we have emergency medications Paul takes when he feels mania is setting in. We know the signs now, but we have to act fast. The WRAP plan is a living document, and we are still making revisions. We take it one day at a time.

* * * * *

Paul's 2021 manic episode, hospitalization, and sudden arrest

In early 2021 one night, Paul drove off in a rage after taking the meds that were supposed to help him, but that really did the opposite. Paul's parents came to stay with us after I saw signs of mania after a ski trip with friends near the anniversary of the first ski accident and his birthday. He had what we would later find out was a paradoxical effect to the emergency medication we were told to administer. We tried for five days to use this medication, but it was having the opposite effect. I hated giving it to him, but his wishes were to stay out of the hospital, and his doctor said to keep trying, it takes time to work sometimes.

After he drove off, we were able to get him escorted by a crisis intervention team in handcuffs to the hospital. I won't go into detail on that, but it was another moment that reshaped who I am as a human. They took him to the hospital to be admitted. It was so cold and I felt like I was gutted. I wore his jacket every day he was gone. I drove his car home in a tearful fog of existence. *Would I ever get him back?* It was the day before Valentine's Day; we had a crazy winter storm. New Mexico still had those crazy strict COVID rules that made things even more closed off to the families, which just added fuel to the fire. I felt hopeless because I couldn't look these professionals in the eyes to let them know we are loving humans and that Paul deserves respect.

I look back at that now, and it is why I made an agreement with God that my new mission is to try to give people the knowledge they need to get respect in the hospitals they entrust the care of their loved ones to. When you are in crisis mode, it is like you are fighting to find your way blindfolded and arms bound. There was no help, and it felt like we were just in free fall.

I went to bed that first night in relative peace because I knew Paul was getting the care he desperately needed. I called at my normal eight-hour mark because I knew when the shift changed for the staff watching over my husband. He was allowed to call me or maybe he just found a phone, but I still have messages from that night. The nurse that answered my call told me my husband had been arrested in the hospital he was trying to get help from . . . I had to peel myself off of the floor. Never in my wildest dreams did I think that would have been possible. So I dove into what I do in crisis mode when I can't do anything else: I research.

I found out that this does indeed happen. It actually happens many times in nursing homes and psychiatric care units. Patients may not go to jail, but they are sued pretty frequently, it seems. There are entire campaigns across the country that call for legislative reform, and people are pushing for better training to help these situations, but there is still so much that needs to be done.

At the time, none of it made any sense. The next few days were such a blur of reality. We were able to get Paul into solitary confinement, which, to this day, I will never know if that was the right thing. There are so many things I question looking back. But there, at least, he supposedly would get his medication.

We were able to gain a course of action with an attorney and got direction on how all of this should work. What blew my mind even more was when they told us that most of the time, after jail, mentally unstable people are let out into parks around downtown because they have no money, no family fighting for them, and no real sense of where they are. It opened my eyes to a reality of society I knew nothing about. So much of my days were mostly praying, crying, and researching. Paul's sister had to leave, and my friend Joyell helped sit with my girls as they attended their online classes, and she taught virtually. It was a nightmare, but I can honestly say light shines in the darkness, and I know who my Earth Angels are. My parents were experiencing life in a record-breaking ice storm in the Austin area, and as soon as they could get to me, they did. It was a blur.

We were able to attend hearings via Zoom, and eventually Paul was released into the care of his dad. He would be at his parents' house, under their care. My parents would help with our needs at our house. We were trying to create normalcy for the girls, but what normalcy could it have been? It was a nightmare, and after jail it was a continuation of a nightmare—and all of it didn't really need to happen. It felt like trauma on top of trauma.

Paul was released from jail a few weeks before our middle daughter's eighth birthday. We had a party for her at Paul's parents' house. Through all of that, we all became so much closer as a family in retrospect, and we were all committed to being the best support system we could for Paul and our girls. I learned—and this was valuable—not to take it personally when I felt like I was to blame for the episodes and their consequences. What could I have done differently to avoid this? What can I do to prevent it from ever happening again? I have to be honest, I still work on that today! I am forever indebted to the love and support of my parents and Paul's parents, his sister, my sister, my brother-in-law, my brother, and a few of my close friends, all supporting me and my daughters.

I could not have gotten through those days without them. When I was completely gutted and couldn't be mommy, they were there for them. This is what any person in crisis needs: a support crew around them.

* * * * *

New realities, having a plan, and today

I always said that when our youngest went to kindergarten I would find my way back to the classroom. I tried working full-time, for two years, but quickly found that our lifestyle requires so much more for me to stay healthy for Paul and our girls. Paul went through many steps, including his own rehab, and all this taught me so much of what it means to take care of my brain and his brain. Brain health is one of the things I am devoted to now; it is foundational.

We were able to shift our sails before I went back to teaching and Paul deeper into real estate. He did residential, and we both started commercial property management after Paul got his real estate license, and we still do that today. Paul still struggled with substance abuse, and I needed to be more present at home, so I did not go back for that third school year. I loved it so much, but I needed to be home.

We took a huge leap and moved to Texas this past Spring. Since moving back to Texas, I am near my family and friends again. For the first time in a long time, I feel we are in a good place where we can see real growth and healing. I attend Al-Anon once a week, and it gives me so much direction and community. It has shown me so much about understanding how I dealt with things in the past and how damaging it was for myself. It has shown me there is another way of loving someone with alcoholism and substance abuse problems. NAMI helps me with the bipolar piece of things. In all the turmoil and lessons that were forced on us at times, we decided we want to help others, and we are working hard to be able to do that. Our system is broken in so many ways, and we aim to help people who are in the same nightmares we have starred in.

This is what any person in crisis needs: hope, a plan, and people around him or her to help that plan become reality. While starting our foundation and writing this book has been healing and has cleared the way for creativity and tangible action, it was also really painful to relive things. It also brought on some depression and relapse for Paul that we are currently working with and through. It brings me to say that therapy is vital to living with someone with bipolar disorder. Being as close to the same page as possible in any marriage is the goal, but therapy gives you that space to do just that. Man, it is not easy, but it is necessary!

Regarding Paul? I have always been in awe of the strength and dignity Paul has in each day I am given with him. He has faced the hard truth that his own brain can turn on him—and it can do so very intensely in ways you don't expect. He works one day at a time to achieve his goals, and I am forever grateful for his love and devotion to learning and becoming better for us and for himself.

Watching him writing this book and starting his foundation has opened up even more love for him I didn't know I had. It is work embodied in something that can live past us. I am so grateful for all the lessons we have learned in this journey. I know I was given this battle to have a perspective on life that I would not have if it wasn't for the moments that felt like rock bottom. I have compassion for this part of the population that gets overlooked, given up on, and even shunned. We have felt the stigma. It hurts the most when you feel it from people you thought were your friends. Even family members sometimes don't get it. We want to bring strength and hope to other people. People don't choose these illnesses. We want to encourage others to give all the information you can to family members and friends; you want to let them do all that they can to help you. We also hope to give them all the "do's and don'ts" we have already troubleshooted for them! I've learned that getting yourself informed is so important.

I don't think I will ever understand why we had to face some of the days that we didn't ask for, but I know it has shaped us into the strong family we have today. It has given all of us strength that we didn't know was possible. Paul is a true warrior, and I am proud to be his partner in this life.

* * * * *

Paul

I will tell you I have always felt a very deep love for Kristen, and we have always been quite affectionate and understood the physical side of a relationship as well. She's going to love that I said that! We have a beautiful relationship today raising our three beautiful daughters, the triple A batteries. Kristen has always made me feel special and surrounded by love.

I like to say this about Kristen: she is *my mirror.* She can see directly into me. She knows when I am doing well and when I am not doing well. She sees the deep defects in my character, even before I do, that will need dealing with.

FIVE

The Game of Golf—and Its Parallels to Life

Let me step away from the current storyline to talk about one of those things that makes life worth living. After all, in the end, we live for the true enjoyments of life, not just work, right?

Like, for instance, golf.

I love the game, and I think it reflects the game of life. But . . . I'll get back to that.

My father introduced me to golf when I was about five, and we had moved to Tampa; we lived in the neighborhood called River Hills. Growing up in this community I had the privilege of living in one of the greatest neighborhoods a child could dream of. I was an avid golfer, even as a boy, and my love of the game became apparent to my parents as young as the age of seven. My parents made huge sacrifices for my sister and me to live in this new community, and they paid for a club membership for me to practice every single day. I had a passion just for being on the driving range.

At a very young age I joined the Greater Tampa Junior Golf Association, and my father and I traveled every month so I could play in junior tournaments. I remember my first golf tournament. I was eight years old and finished in third place.

As the community around us grew, I made new friends in Kevin and Kyle Adkins. As kids we were inseparable. We would play other sports such as basketball, tennis, football, roller hockey, soccer, baseball, swimming, and just about anything that had a ball. My two favorite sports, though, were definitely golf and basketball. During my time at River Hills Country Club I would win three junior club championships and have the honor and privilege of being invited to play at the famous Pinehurst golf complex in North Carolina. I got to play Pinehurst No. 1 in the junior North-South Championship.

I was quite the athlete growing up as a kid. At the age of 14 I was being recruited by high school teams across Central Florida. At that age my dream was to be a professional golfer. I had a six handicap, and my only real sports thought was that as I got older I would continue practicing until I become one of the best golfers in the world. Like many kids, I would imagine making the final putt to win the most famous golf tournament in the world, the Masters.

One of my childhood friends, who was also a great golfer, was Ty Tryon. He would attend one of my birthday parties, held on the golf course. Well, Ty would go on to become the youngest junior golfer to make the PGA Tour at the amazingly young age of 17. Before that, of course, we competed together in Greater Tampa Junior Golf events for many years, and I always admired Ty's golf game.

When our family decided to move to Texas, I would eventually make the golf team at The Woodlands High School. The competition became more fierce, way more competitive, with about sixty or more kids on the golf team. And although I made the varsity team my junior year in high school and was one of the better kids on the team, there was a freshman, Bronson Burgoon, who I could never beat.

Still, golf always captivated me. In the summer of 2001, just before my senior year in high school, there was a guy named Tiger Woods who would shoot 21 under par at the famous Saint Andrews course in Scotland to win the British Open. I've always found it a beautiful sport, and this kid named Tiger, just 25 years old, made it even more so.

So there were really good players around me. Maybe I was burned out a bit. Probably, I was; I had been playing, a lot, for a dozen years. For whatever reasons exactly, I decided to quit the game before my high school senior year. But I watched as Bronson went on to become a collegiate golfer at Texas A&M and later receive his PGA Tour card.

Still, I believe the game has always remained in my blood.

Do I regret quitting competitive golf? I can't say that exactly, but I will say that when I finished college I wished I had tried to play at the collegiate level.

Today, I play about two to three times a week. I love trying to beat my previous scores. Golf is an interesting game that has many amateurs borderline-addicted. Some people would say playing two to three times a week is a lot of golf. Others would say that isn't very much in their book!

I play a lot with my dad, when we can. My dad likes to say that he lets me beat him most of the time, but it isn't true.

* * * * *

In my opinion golf is one of the greatest games ever invented. Golf is very similar to life. In fact, I'll go further: golf is exactly like life! You take one day at a time, just like you take one shot at a time. You're going to have good days, and good shots. You're going to find yourself staring at bad days, and bad shots. But you keep looking forward; you can't change yesterday, and you can't change the last shot. You forget about the bad shot just behind you and move on.

Golf is also like life in this way. Sometimes we get good breaks with our bad shots, and sometimes we get bad breaks with even excellent shots. It's very similar, of course, in life with the breaks—for good and bad—that we get. In life we take shots with our career, our family, our social network, where we decide to live, where we go to college, who we decide to date or get married to, whether to have children or not have kids—in short, what we want to do with our lives.

Many choices that we make in our lives . . . well, we can't always get them back. The bottom line is we have to move on, keep going in the journey of life. And golf is a lot like that.

You can start a round very poorly and then have a stretch of absolutely great holes. Or, it can go the other way.

Regardless of the choices we make in life, we have to live with them and move on. We'll have positive consequences and negative consequences.

Which is a lot like a round of golf.

SIX

Serving the Deathcare Industry

When my father grew up in Wilmington, Delaware, he went to a Catholic school named Saint Mark's High School. But when he was not in school, he was working at Silverbrook Cemetery. He started working there at a young age painting the outside fence. He would later move on to cutting grass, trimming memorials and headstones, fixing irrigation lines, planting trees, installing monuments, and, of course, the usual digging of graves and setting up for funeral services in the cemetery.

About the time my dad graduated high school, his father moved the family to Bloomfield, New Mexico, where my grandfather had just taken a job as an electrical engineer at a power plant. So my dad, as a very young man, now needed to find new work. The first job he found, and took, was laying concrete.

Later, as I said earlier, he became a Bloomfield policeman and met my mother at the restaurant. That led to my parents living in a mobile home, my dad watching other friends on the force die, having to work the Santa Fe prison riots, and more, leaving them to move back to Wilmington, Delaware.

After the years in Wilmington—my dad worked his way to general manager of the cemetery—he took the job in Corpus Christi, Texas. But my introduction to the funeral and cemetery industry was yet to come. That was in the fall of 1990; I was just seven and we were living, as I wrote earlier, in Florida.

I was going to be starting the second grade. My father and I would commute to Tampa every morning. I remember it vividly because we would leave around 5:30 and stop at a Shell station for gas, donuts, and coffee and listen to oldies music as we drove into Tampa. I thought it was the coolest thing to see my father dressed up in a suit and tie and driving a white 1990 Oldsmobile company car.

After school he would pick me up around 2:30 and bring me back to the funeral home and cemetery. When I got to the funeral home I was able to meet a lot of the staff inside and outside the cemetery. I didn't fully understand, at that stage of life, what my dad did for his career (what kid does?). All I really knew was that when somebody died, my dad knew what to do and how to take care of families.

He had a strong, hard work ethic with an incredible amount of discipline not to let what happened at work affect his mood at home. Growing up, I never saw my father lose his temper with my mom or sister. He was always calm and collected. He taught me that, although he wore a suit and tie to work every day, to be respected one must remain humble. He also taught me that everything that seems to be a challenge is only going to be a temporary situation. He taught me that relationships are very important, and trust is what builds true character. And he taught me that you will make many choices and decisions in life, and it is your job to own each and every one.

All this I was learning as a young boy, but I had some experiences in that setting, too. After school one day, after he brought me back to the funeral home, my father told me I could explore anywhere in that home—except for the chapel. It was kind of like—you guessed it, from the Bible—"you can eat from any tree, but don't eat from *that* tree." So, naturally, as a 7-year-old the only thought that ran through my mind was: "What's in the chapel?"

I waited until I was sure nobody was watching me, and then my only mission was to make it into that chapel. As I opened the door I noticed a casket was open and that someone's loved one was laid out in the middle of that room. This was my first experience seeing a dead body, but it would definitely not be the last. I remember it like yesterday. The woman was wearing a blue dress, she was an African-American, and her name was Miss Williams. There is no experience quite like that for a 7-year-old; the image remains in my mind. But also, I think I experienced the serenity and respect of death, that each person has an innate dignity even after their passing.

As the year went on I would go back to the funeral home and hear stories from workers about different families and tasks that needed to be taken care of. I learned a lot of the terminology of the industry and met a lot of good people who cared about their jobs. I came to a point of, even more deeply, admiring the work my father did.

Another experience from the funeral home: one time there was a military individual laid out in the chapel with full dress military uniform. When the family arrived at 5 PM for a private visitation, they realized that the uniform name was correct, as was the proper uniform and decorations and medals, but all of them were on the wrong body! The hospital staff had put the wrong ankle tag on the wrong body. Needless to say, though the funeral home had not been the one to make the mistake, you learn the care with which you must address, and apologize for, such an error. At that moment every person in the funeral home got to work to make sure to take that uniform off the decedent's body and then work to discover what had happened. As it turned out, the loved one they were looking for was at a different funeral home.

In 1996 (I'm 13) our family decided to move to Houston, Texas. My dad would take a job with Carriage Services as one of their vice presidents of operations. He commuted an hour and a half every day to work and typically traveled Monday through Thursday to visit other firms and employees. My dad worked in that position for five years until he decided to resign in the summer of 2000.

As part of his severance package he was restricted from working in any funeral home or cemetery in the U.S. for at least one year. But during that year he would take on consulting jobs in Central America and travel frequently to provide support and guidance to international funeral homes and cemeteries.

In 2001 Service Corp. International had recently acquired several funeral homes, cemeteries, and crematories in the state of New Mexico. My parents often thought of going back to New Mexico since my mom's family still lived there. So my father took a job as an area operational manager and moved to Albuquerque my senior year in high school while the rest of the family stayed in Houston.

This was an incredible opportunity for our family, and one of the best decisions my family ever made. As a senior in high school I decided to apply for the University of New Mexico so that, when I finished school, I would move to Albuquerque for college. It was a dream for my parents to move back to New Mexico, but it would take four years for the entire family to be back in Albuquerque. My sister Jessica was a junior in high school and my parents did not want to move her during her senior year in high school. My mother had a full-time job as an international ticket counter agent for Continental Airlines in Houston. With flight benefits from my mom's job, my father would frequently travel back and forth from Albuquerque to Houston to visit us on the weekends.

My dad took a huge risk to move again in his life. One thing I knew for certain was that the funeral home and cemetery industry had always provided for our family. My entire childhood, youth, and way of living is a testament to my father's hard work and dedication to the profession.

With this in mind, I decided to attend the University of New Mexico with no intention other than to work with my dad after graduating. During my four years in college I would work part-time learning all the different roles and responsibilities within the funeral home and cemetery business.

I earned a bachelor's degree in organizational communication and also had an emphasis on Spanish. I received a minor in entrepreneurial studies and marketing from the Anderson School Business and Administration. I was fascinated with, in particular, organizational communication. My father managed more than 200 employees, and I knew that managing people, processes, and systems would be my choice in college. Organizational communication studies also teaches leadership styles and how to set the culture in any organization so that the business remains productive and on task without losing focus of its vision and goals.

* * * * * * *

In the fall of 2002, I remember when I was told I would be reporting to Vista Verde Memorial Park and Funeral Home for the very first time that I would be cutting grass. I was also told I would be working with Moon and Wayne. I would report to Jim, and he would give me instructions. I thought I would be driving a lawn mower. When I arrived I was told to cut, mow, and trim the Garden of Innocence.

This particular section of the cemetery, well, it was forbidden to use the riding mower. This section was (and is) one of the most sacred sections in the entire cemetery; it's where babies and infants are laid to rest. The work required using a push mower along with moving all the decorations and trinkets from each and every grave in order to trim the headstones. The job was a little overwhelming but, at the same time, quite rewarding. I was definitely overwhelmed by the number of infants and babies laid to rest in the cemetery, not to mention that there was a lot of grass to be cut with a simple push mower!

This work, though, taught me a great deal: the human touch needed, the personal touch, the importance in the lives of parents and families. An innocent child has lost its life. It might be a cliché, but it seems so true: a parent shouldn't have to bury their own child.

I went on to learn so much more. After completing cutting the grass in the Garden of Innocence, I would move on to learn installing headstones. This particular job was fascinating in that it required measurements and precise locations for installation. Not to mention that we had to make sure that the monument was going on the proper grave. I learned very quickly about the different sections in the cemetery and what were lots, blocks, and grave spaces in every single section. Installing monuments and headstones is a tough job as these things are extremely heavy and hard to move even with a dolly and two men.

Still more to learn: maintaining the beauty of a cemetery is an extremely challenging job. Not to mention that we dig graves by hand along with operating a backhoe. Digging a grave with a backhoe was a fascinating thing to learn and experience. I remember watching Moon dig the first grave, and I couldn't believe what I saw under the ground. There had to be five vaults with loved ones laid to rest underground, and we were responsible for digging a grave that was 40 inches wide by 8 feet long and, of course, 6 feet deep. Sometimes you would even dig "double depth"—or 8 feet deep—for companion graves. And you had to be mindful of irrigation lines underground and monuments all over the cemetery.

After opening up a grave we would set up the casket-lowering device, put up a tent, the greens, and chairs so that when the funeral home and its guests arrived we would be ready to lower the casket soon after final services. Of course, we're responsible for making sure that the pallbearers place the casket on top of the lowering device in a safe manner and in no danger that it would slip off into the earth.

After a graveside service we would lower the casket, backfill the grave, and lay all the appropriate flowers that had been there for the funeral.

During my senior year in college, 2006, I passed my life and health insurance exam and became a licensed life insurance agent to sell pre-need life insurance. After graduating from the University of New Mexico I would join the family service sales department and would continue on this path for four years with twenty-five other agents who worked for the funeral homes and cemeteries. There were many mentors I was gifted with during this time in my life, but the two who I want to give special mention to are Alan Birchfield and Steve Simko.

I was extremely excited to attend sales meetings held by the sales manager Alan Birchfield who was so passionate about sales and marketing. I would soak up as much information from him every day. He was so committed to the sales profession within the funeral and cemetery industry. He said sales is an art and science and you are the artist. I was officially a professional salesman.

Afterwards, in 2010 I would obtain my funeral directors licence where I was an apprentice funeral director under Steve Simko. I was then responsible for meeting with families to make funeral, burial, and cremation arrangements and direct funerals for families. As a licensed funeral director for many years of my life, I helped thousands of families across New Mexico say goodbye to their loved ones with professionalism and grace. I was dedicated to the profession.

Due to a variety of reasons our family decided to sell the funeral and cemetery businesses in New Mexico and move on from the heartfelt traumas of working with bereaved families of loved ones each and every day. It became and still is today an engraved part of my identity. The trauma is something I am still working through, but the rewards that the funeral profession brought to my life are immeasurable, and I am so blessed it was a huge part of my story. Funeral service is a ministry, but is extremely time constrictive, twenty-four seven, three hundred sixty-five days a year, and exhausting. It was time to move on.

SEVEN

Life after the Deathcare Profession

After fourteen years of working in the funeral and cemetery industry (2002-2016), my father came home from a trip to Mexico City with a box of dog toys. I asked him a simple question: "Why do you have so many dog toys, and you don't even own a dog?"

He asked if I wanted to try them out on my dog Roxy. The toys were great; they were made of a durable natural rubber with a hole in them so you could put treats in them. There were four different sizes, and there were also different toys with ropes on them. Roxy and I would play fetch, and I tell you for certain they were extremely durable when played with.

I asked my dad where these toys came from. He mentioned the name of a man I respected very much: Nemesio. This man was like a brother to my father.

Turns out, the family I lived with in Mexico City when I was 15 wanted to offer our family an opportunity to bring their brand of toys to the U.S. and Canada.

The family had ties with relatives who owned a rubber plant in Mexico City. The name of the factory was Grupo 201, and it had been in operation since 1945. They also made tennis balls and other equipment for the sports manufacturer Wilson, and they were just getting into the pet toy industry. They started calling their new line 4BF: For Best Friends. Their dream was to take these products north of the border into the U.S. and Canada.

My father let me know the principal person was Nemesio's niece and nephew Adrianna and Rodrigo Ledesma. They invited me down there, and I ended up heading down and exploring the factory in Mexico; they had hundreds of products. Dad and I had no experience at all with these products or this industry, but we made the trip to tour the factory. Nemesio was our host and guide during the tour.

In short, the products were brought to the U.S., and they had reached as many as 1300 stores (in 40 states), including Petco stores, by the time the Covid pandemic hit in 2020. 4BF was going strong, but then the business growth was stopped entirely by the pandemic. Grupo 201's factory in Mexico city was closed for more than nine months. In a really short amount of time, that business was gone.

By the end of 2020 I had to get out of the pet toy business. I was learning to deal with bad situations and making sure I didn't relapse.

My next stop was the real estate business.

In 2003 during my time at the University of New Mexico I met a student named Joseph Maez at the Anderson School of Business Administration in a marketing class. After leaving the pet toy business I reached out to Joe in 2020. I needed something different. Joe told me to get my real estate license. During the summer of 2020, at the beginning of the Covid 19 pandemic, I studied for two months to take the National Association of Realtors licensing exam. After passing the exam I would join the Maez Group and start selling houses.

I was always fascinated with Joe and his real estate profession. Today I am still close with Joe, but consider myself more of a commercial landlord. Today I manage a commercial building in Corrales, New Mexico that has nineteen occupied tenants.

I have learned so much from him, and he worked closely with my wife and dad when I experienced mania. We are all very grateful for his understanding and respect.

EIGHT

Bipolar Disorder and Alcoholism: The Accident, the After-Effects

My sophomore year at the University of New Mexico was the year I was diagnosed with Bipolar Disorder 1 with acute mania.

To understand this better, bipolar disorder has different forms: 1 is distinguished from, and more intense than, Bipolar Disorder 2. It is important to figure out which one you have to help in your recovery. Well, I can speak from experience in telling you, it matters and helps tremendously to understand your diagnosis.

Bipolar 1 is characterized by an intense, persistent mood elevation period lasting at least one week, and it is often accompanied by symptoms such as inflated self-esteem, decreased need for sleep, racing thoughts, impulsivity, and risky behavior. Bipolar 2 has many of the same symptoms, but it is milder in intensity and causes less impairment in daily functioning. Both, though, can involve depressive episodes characterized by sadness, loss of interest, fatigue, worthlessness, and even thoughts of suicide. Bipolar 1 is less common than Bipolar 2. Bipolar 1 can lead to severe manic episodes. Bipolar 2 can lead to frequent and even prolonged depressive episodes.

Before I was diagnosed, I went on a ski trip with several of my friends to Breckenridge, Colorado in January 2004. We ended up staying there for four nights. The now well-known Winter Sports X Games had just completed their competition, and the stunt park was still open for visitors.

On the second day, my good buddy Jasper and I decided to explore the park. We were absolutely amazed by the size of the place—and the size of some of the jumps we thought we could make. Jasper was a snowboarder while I preferred to ski. For two days Jasper and I would ski and board together . . . and, of course, we made our way to the stunt park.

Somehow, I thought it was a good idea to add sangria wine to my camelback. As 20-year-old college kids we thought we were on top of the world and unstoppable on the slopes. Neither of us were wearing helmets, and we were taking some incredibly dangerous jumps and giving virtually no thought to ever getting hurt. I am convinced the wine wasn't all of the reason I crashed, but it wasn't the right choice, either. Your inhibitions quickly get swept away. I know it surely had some effect, and it's not hard to see now I shouldn't have had it in my camelback.

On the last day of our trip—in fact, one of our last afternoons runs—I pushed the limit a bit too far. The height of the ramp was about 8 feet, and to clear the tabletop you had to go at a pretty good speed to catch the landing area. I decided as one of the last runs I'd go at full speed, which is about 25 miles an hour.

Jasper went first, and he landed. At full speed I attempted the jump and found myself going too fast when I hit the take-off. Keep in mind, I had no helmet. My head was in front of my feet . . .

The next thing I remember is waking up in the emergency room at a Breckenridge hospital.

Jasper told me I had been convulsing, shaking, foaming at the mouth, and literally unconscious at the bottom of the slope. They told me later I was likely unconscious for a full 15 minutes. I can't imagine the trauma this put Jasper through. He proceeded to call the paramedics while staying with me, and I was taken down the mountain in a sleigh. To this day I'm extremely grateful Jasper was my skiing partner, because I truly believe he saved my life.

Being taken down that mountain in that sled, I remember them holding up fingers and asking me how many. This was the first of many, many memories of injury and recovery. I remember my ski goggles were still on, and I could feel that my shoulder was in great pain. Likely, I instinctively tried to land on the shoulder area to protect my head. (To this day, my shoulder is pretty messed up.)

I was admitted to the nearest hospital in Breckinridge that could handle this kind of trauma. For two weeks my shoulder was in so much pain I could not lay down to sleep. I was harnessed in a sling and had to sleep upright.

I think it was the day after the accident that I was discharged—with plenty of pain meds and a sling. Fraternity brothers had driven up from Albuquerque for this ski trip. They drove me back to Albuquerque.

My birthday is February 4th, and the accident happened about 10 days before. So this was my twenty-first birthday, and it wasn't a good one.

I was on the pain meds, of course, but I took cocaine during this time, drank, and had blackouts. I even went on what was basically a two-week bender, and it seems those first four to five weeks were chaotic.

I didn't make it through the academic semester; I had to disenroll from classes.

In March, after a prolonged period of not being able to sleep, and people noticing plenty of things wrong with me, I was admitted into psychiatric care. And I think I was having plenty of paranoia.

So I was hospitalized for a few days and placed on tranquilizer meds so I could sleep. I think I was there for about four to five days and, no surprise, I gained weight. I recall I was even locked up in a room for three to four days. When I went home, I was assigned a psychiatrist.

I met with that doctor weekly. He adjusted my meds and told me that, in no uncertain terms, I had to stop any drugs and all alcohol. And this period went on for another five, six months.

After this time, I would have occasional alcohol, but no drugs. I re-enrolled for school in the fall of 2004, and did quite well academically.

But I was also newly diagnosed with a traumatic brain injury (commonly known as a TBI). I had a hard time remaining in the habit of taking my needed medications. It was during this time that I was diagnosed with the bipolar condition, and I was given different meds to try during this time. Some of the manic actions I described in the first chapter were starting to show themselves at this time.

Still, I worked hard to get into a routine, and by the end of 2004 and into 2005 I was working very hard at my med schedule. I worked more at the cemetery and funeral business, I moved into an off-campus apartment with a good roommate, and I became very good at studying. In short, I was balanced and stable for 2005.

The work at the cemetery was going very well for me. In two years I was able to finish school and get my undergraduate degree. I remember it felt like a bit of a race to get through school, but I did it.

I would travel to Texas A&M to visit Kristen. (She did come visit me in the immediate period after the ski accident.) In 2005 I spent a good deal of time that year seeking to reconnect with Kristen. She was fully supportive of me, and I like to say that she kept me "steady as she goes."

But when you have these sorts of conditions, things aren't perfect. I had a setback with some binge drinking during my final semester. I probably had too much time on my hands. By 2006 Kristen and I were living together—she had moved to Albuquerque after graduating A&M. But I kept coming home later and showing other bad behaviors.

She changed the locks on the apartment and kicked me out.

Following that, I lived with my parents in Albuquerque and finished school in fall 2006.

Kristen and I got back together around October 2006, but I was still drinking—too much. At the same time, I was making a number of steps forward in life. In November of that year I got my life insurance license to sell funeral product. So, come 2007, I was off to the races in my sales training and writing contracts.

It's easy to see how things can run in cycles: now I slowed my drinking because I was so busy with work. But then came another huge mistake.

In October 2007 I was charged with Driving Under the Influence (DUI). This was a Wednesday night, and I remember it well. After being pulled over, I was booked into jail on DUI. That is a huge embarrassment and shameful experience. But life has to go on.

In the summer of 2007 I was able to purchase my first house. I had proposed to Kristen in March of that year in Cadiz, Spain. But I was still making mistakes. I was still drinking even while I thought I was a controlled drinker.

Kristen and I were married on June 14, 2008, one of my best days ever. And I spent most of 2008 alcohol-free.

As you can see, that is a quite a journey from 2004 to 2008, and many things happened along that way.

* * * * *

In the years that followed, I had more struggles. But the biggest memory, and what took a lot of effort and emotion (along with working full-time), I became a father.

In 2010, I became a father for the first time. I experienced a love I never knew existed. When I saw and held my first daughter, I could not stop crying. It felt like a flood of every emotion I had ever experienced in my life. I was so happy I was a dad, but also terrified. There is a lot of work that goes into parenting three children—

all girls—at young ages. Work, yes, but so much joy, a great deal of joy.

There are many different challenges to this day, but the joy always surpasses them. My daughters are Annelise (15), Adelynn (13), and Ava (10). Kristen worked until we had the first baby, but then we decided she would stay home. She was and still is the most attentive, patient mother I have ever met in my life. I can tell in her eyes she just loves being a mom. Across these very young years for my girls, I worked in the funeral business, then 4BF, as I wrote about in the earlier chapter. They loved being a part of the dog toy business. We all had fun with it, so it was really sad when we had to close.

* * * * *

By 2019 my therapist, Michael, eventually recommended I attend Cottonwood, in Tucson, Arizona, for rehabilitation.

Why did I go along with making the steps to carry out this recommendation? I didn't like how I felt. I was taking my medication, seeing my psychiatrist, and now I had been seeing Michael for two to three years at that point. I was angry and bitter at where I was in life. I was mad I was someone who struggles with bipolar disorder, and I was self-medicating. I always felt like I was missing out on a life that was taken from me in so many ways by this illness. I wasn't in a healthy mindset at all.

Michael was pretty strong in his recommendation that, "You need to go to rehabilitation." There was no single event, no "aha" moment. It was a series of things that had built and built for years. I respect his opinion so much, too.

Like I said, I had been seeing Michael for two to three years. I trusted him when he made such a strong recommendation. It helped that he was someone I had known for more than two years. I looked at him as a credible source. I could trust that he had my best interests at heart. He cared about my wellbeing and wanted to see me better. There's also this: he didn't recommend just any place, or just to "go to rehab." He specifically recommended Cottonwood Tucson, and I couldn't be happier that he did.

One of the first things was discussing this possibility with Kristen and my parents. They were all very supportive.

I'm proud of this: I'm the one who booked the visit, contacted Cottonwood, made the first payment, scheduled, scheduled transportation, all of that.

It was an investment of thousands, and my insurance paid for half, which helped tremendously. (I am grateful for that.) One of the things I want to do with my foundation, the Alive Now Foundation, is to help with scholarships to help fund rehabilitation for others. Insurance is a great help, so people want to be aware of what coverage they do have or could get.

Was it hard to get myself out there, get off that plane, get to the center, and across that threshold? I guess that answer is yes, but looking back, I have a lot of joy in the memory. I knew it was a huge step in getting healthy.

There are always costs and hurdles with something like this. I did feel nervous about leaving my wife and small girls (9, 6, and 4 at the time), but Kristen's parents, my in-laws, stepped up to help with the girls, and that meant a great deal and helped with feeling that they would be secure. They did have some family days where Kristen, the girls, and our parents came. Kristen and my parents took classes and went to therapy sessions with me. Kristen learned so much more about my illness and was given more resources to help me, which she loved, and still references her binder to this day.

I arrived at Cottonwood September 19, 2019.

I would stay there for 30 days, completing my rehabilitation on October 19, 2019. Since that date I've also learned so much to maintain sobriety and live a better life today. Bipolar disorder and the addicted brain tend to be pretty sneaky and lie a lot, but I am still learning to listen to my higher power, to act from my higher self and wise brain. Sometimes that wise brain gets lost, and that is what I have to fight for one day at a time.

NINE

Cottonwood, and Recovery

During my time at Cottonwood rehabilitation in Tucson, I learned that every individual who attended there had been, and likely still was, going through something big in their life—and the only way they had known to cope with their issues was to turn to drugs, alcoholism, or some form of addiction that altered their state of mind.

There are a number of critical things that I learned about recovery, and these will be important to any person entering this journey.

I found that it needs to be viewed as done in a safe place. No technology, no distractions. It is all about human connections. For us in Cottonwood, there was regular care and meetings, and we truly built a common bond. The bond? That every last one of us would get well, and we believed in each other.

There were about fifty people in the program at the time I was there, and they were from all over the world.

We would get up early and have breakfast together. It was like a community of broken people, all trying to get well. After a long day, lights would go out at between 9 and 10 PM.

My roommate for three of the four weeks I was in there was a guy from Chicago. His name is Jim and he suffered from alcoholism. We developed a great bond. The only way to keep that bond was to attend the AA meetings.

We would have breakout sessions with speakers, workout sessions, art classes, guided meditation, and more. The workshops would deal with addictions, alcoholism, and recovery. I started reading what they call "The Big Book of AA." Praying, meditating, working out, and eating and sleeping well were all stressed.

The center focused on lower-stress situations, and this is needed as one continues their recovery. It is where you have to start getting yourself out of the perpetual loops that are so easy to get trapped in.

Another huge thing I learned was acceptance—of yourself. You've got to expect in life that, at times, things aren't going to go your way. You have to learn to surround yourself with support people. Of course, as I have said, Kristen is my starting point there.

Back to the center: I would meet one-on-one with an advisor, but the biggest part of it was group sessions. I did many of the activities with Jim.

Jim had a great saying I've not forgotten, and I keep living by it: "You don't graduate from recovery. You just graduate from the rehab center."

You also learn you're not alone in this world. You're not the only one struggling with mental health and addictions. You find that your development is kind of an evolution of sorts:

- You begin to see that you can shed things in your life that you don't need;
- You increasingly learn you can't control everything; you have to accept that many things are outside of your control;
- You begin to learn that you are far from alone. Others will face very similar circumstances. Others will need to go through recovery processes very much like yours.

During recovery, I began taking a mood stabilizer medication and an anti-psychotic medication. I am still on those meds today. I also have at my disposal an emergency tranquilizer, but it knocks me out for 12 hours, so I use it sparingly. I may go a full year without taking it. THC use had me rapid cycling and I didn't realize it. I had to take it a few times when mania was inching in.

I also felt like I needed it to mellow out. Turns out I didn't need it at all. The hard part is that mania feels so good too. Having Kristen and our Wellness Recovery Action Plan has kept me the most stable. I have been on all these meds for close to twenty years. I know some people never find the right prescription, and I am so lucky I found mine.

More things I learned at Cottonwood:

- You can relate to nearly everyone else in some way. Whether it is PTSD (post-traumatic stress disorder), depression, bipolar, alcoholism, or drug addiction . . . there are common threads.

- Everyone is in there for the same reason: to get well and live a better, productive life.

- Again, like Jim said, you don't "graduate" from recovery; you complete the Cottonwood program.

- I learned there is a community of people who are my fellow recoverees. They, like me, "live today." There's a fellowship of people I have remained friends with to this day, and I surround myself with them in different ways to stay in recovery.

- If you choose to continue to attend regular AA meetings, it is easier to tell yourself that recovery is a choice, and you are making it every day.

TEN

The Power of Community

There is a real fellowship with Alcoholics Anonymous, and the continuation of practicing the steps has shown itself to be the best work I can do in my recovery. My personality meshes well with the routine and structure. I have met some of the best people in those rooms. You go into a room with 15 to 30, or more, people—I've been in meetings with nearly 80 to 100 people—and you recognize the faces and you know their names if it is one of your home groups . . . Well, when you sit with them in a room for an hour and you share a common illness—yes, it's an illness, and there are often mental health issues too—that's what I love most about AA. Even when I travel, I find AA meetings to help myself. There is a fellowship and you don't feel alone. The Big Book of AA is about 164 pages, and as people share from it and from a particular topic, and share about their lives—there is so much more than just sharing about alcohol and drugs. Really, they are sharing about *life*.

We realize we have common questions: how am I overcoming my challenges? How are we dealing with life? What am I *grateful* for? What are you struggling with, whether it's parenting, marriage, drugs, alcohol, jobs, or career? You realize there is a lot that people in recovery are dealing with, but you realize, really, we're all human. All people face these challenges. So we are part of the same struggle even though we have these addictions to overcome.

It's therapeutic for each person to share, and then you can relate. You sit there and think, *Oh, yeah, I could see how that would suck. . . .* Or, *I could see how that would be great.* Just to hear people's stories: if their kids are graduating, how life is going, becomes some of the best parts of your day. I've come to this viewpoint: current events that a friend in group is dealing with, well, that's more important to me than what's on the news today. Or, what's the hot topic in culture? That means very little to me compared with sharing life with my fellow recoverees.

Here's an example of what I mean. Bob, an elderly man, shares his story from about thirty years ago: someone broke into his home. That intruder attacked his elderly mother, raped her, and killed her. He shares about how traumatic the event was, but here was his great discovery. He said: "I realized I didn't have to drink over that situation, because it wouldn't have solved any of the problems." I thought about that, and I realized: he got through that event without having to drink himself to death, or to drink at all. I have never forgotten Bob's story; I remember that evening vividly. He got sober around 30 years of age and stayed with AA all those years—including through that severely traumatic time.

For me? I often share about the journey of parenting. I like to say that, "This is the first time I've been a parent to daughters who are 15, 12, and 10." I mean, I've never been here before, you know? I have to learn to have an emotional balance, to keep my emotions in check. I have to learn to walk away, or to call another alcoholic, or another friend, who is in the program. "Listen: this is what's going on."

Those friends tend to understand that you are vulnerable. To just call someone and say, "How do I handle this moment?" And to hear the person on the other end say, "It's okay. It's temporary. It's going to be okay." Sometimes, that's all you need—just to hear from another friend in the program. I'll do that a couple of times a month, easily. I like to call it the "phone-a-friend" line.

* * * * *

So what are meetings like? I'll be honest: the first 15 minutes are probably like every meeting in the world: there's always the standard stuff, a sort of ritual. So, you realize there's ritual, but you're okay with that. (Again,

I've seen meetings with 70 to 100 people, and I've seen meetings with just six or seven.) The meeting chairman picks a topic, and people share what is relevant to them, what helps them with recovery.

There are meetings with different formats: open meetings for friends and family without any addictions, who are welcome to come and support; closed meetings are *only* for those who are seeking to overcome an addiction, men only and female only. I go to the meetings usually four to five times a week, four easily: Sunday, Tuesday, Friday, Saturday. I do prefer the men-only meetings. I go to about half that are open and half that are closed. There are also dual-recovery meetings: these are meetings of those with both mental illness and an alcohol or drug addiction. I am part of this community as well, though it is not a large group, percentagewise, among all of us who are in AA.

Meetings last one hour, and it's not uncommon for a dozen or even more people to share. You share for about three minutes each; that's supposed to be the limit.

The first time I told my full story of being incarcerated and realizing there was a mental illness, I broke down and wept. But it's therapeutic to speak the words. When I think back, it's still very impactful to think about being in solitary confinement, and naked, and helpless. I told that story, and it helped a lot of people. It can be emotional sometimes, for sure. It helps to put the thoughts, the words, down. Even doing this book has been therapeutic for me. It also feels amazing when you hear that your pain helped someone deal with theirs.

Really, for me, the go-to formula is "one day at a time," which is why that's part of the title of this book. That's one of the prime things AA has taught me: it's just one day at a time. Take it one day at a time. It's also the name of a song written by Los Tigres del Norte "Un Dia a La Vez"—translated to "one day at a time" in Spanish, from 1981. For those of you who listen to Mexican music by Los Tigres del Norte, I encourage you to listen to the lyrics as they were one of the inspirations for writing this book.

I often get asked if AA ever seems repetitive or "gets old." Not really. There are different topics each time, but there are different people of all types, and you never know what is going to be shared and how it might help you. You go to offer "experience, strength, or hope"—and hopefully if you're not in a good space, someone else will offer you experience, strength, and hope. That's another one of my key sayings about being a part of such a community: you're there to share and offer experience, strength, and hope. Really—not to be funny—but it's somewhat like what people look for in going to a bar. They're looking for a social setting where they can be accepted.

Plain and simple, it is a community of broken people trying to feel whole. There's a sign someone put up: "We're all crazy, and it's not a competition." I like that.

Sometimes people like to tell their drunk stories, like, "I've done this," or, "I've done that," and almost boast like, "I'm more sick than you are." You have to come to realize: we're all the same. You may have been at one place, and I've been at another, but we're really all the same. It's not a competition. I am no better than the homeless drug addict on the side of the road; none of us are.

* * * * *

One of the things that gives me great strength is the Serenity Prayer. Chances are you've seen it, somewhere, presented in some way:

God grant me the serenity
To accept the things I cannot change;
Courage to change the things I can;
And wisdom to know the difference.

This is my favorite prayer that I've ever gotten from AA. In my opinion, it's the best prayer on planet Earth. I think about it a lot. It's also the opening prayer to every AA meeting.

Here is another organization that offers mental health support: NAMI (National Association for Mental Illness). There are also initiatives like Care not Cuffs that are fighting for the end to arresting individuals who are seeking medical care.

AA insists on belief in a Higher Power, and this can be the God of your choice or own understanding—but yes, most people apply this to God, the God of the Bible. AA is not a religious program, but it is spiritual. What is my higher power? I believe in God, and Christianity. (I don't endorse or have to be a part of any denomination or anything like that.) But also a large part of my spiritual journey is AA itself: reading The Big Book, going to meetings, praying, and meditating. I'll be honest: I also like Hinduism and like to hold to some of its principles. I appreciate a lot of things about the Hindu faith. In short, I'm a Christian who believes in Hinduism as well.

It's important that everybody has some type of higher power. To me, it doesn't matter if it's Christianity or Hinduism or Buddhism or Islam—just something in which you realize: *I'm not God.*

Of the AA famous 12 steps, the only one you have to embrace is the first one. As I go through a few of these, I'll put them in my words, as I view them, versus the official AA wording. It is great to search these also, if you wish, and please do.

The first step: admitting you're powerless over alcohol and that your life is unmanageable. If you don't get that one right, nothing else will matter.

I like to say that alcoholism is the only disease in which you have to diagnose yourself; no one is going to diagnose it for you. I use that quote a lot in meetings. A doctor, or family member, or loved one: they can't truly diagnose you. They can point you in the right direction, but you have to diagnose this. The rest is garbage if you can't accept this yourself.

Second is coming to an understanding that until you accept a power higher than yourself, you remain in insanity. That's accepting a *big thing:* that you're insane. These two steps follow each other; they are in order for a reason.

Third: you make a decision to turn your will and your life over to the care of your God as you understand him. So you believe and you make a decision. It's that simple, in one sense, but that crucial, and that powerful.

I'll skip to the last step of the 12: having had a spiritual awakening, as a result of those steps, we seek to carry forward these principles and practice them in all of our affairs. That last one: I've committed it to memory. It's very important.

* * * * *

Another part of my recovery process was being certified as a peer support worker. This particular certification requires at least three years of sobriety, other requirements, and taking an exam to be certified. I completed my certification in February of 2024. As I work on this book in late fall 2025, though, I have not yet used that certification. I never got a particular job, or a chance to use it. It seems wild to me that it will soon be two years since receiving that. Maybe that will change and I'll be able to use it; we'll see. But going through that process was valuable and helpful. Since moving to Texas, the New Mexico certification is not eligible. In time, I might be able to get the same in Texas.

* * * * *

As someone who lives with a mental illness of bipolar disorder, with alcoholism, and with post-traumatic stress disorder, Alcoholics Anonymous (AA), therapy, and taking my medications have been the best tools to maintain my sobriety.

I've met so many wonderful people in the AA program. Many of whom I consider really good friends. Listening to their stories of how they recovered and who they were in their past has taught me that I'm not alone, and that recovery is possible. This is why it's been a blessing to continue to attend regular meetings after being discharged from Cottonwood Tucson.

When I experience mania, I get obsessive over "doubling my recovery efforts." I have to be mindful and remember my home and my family too. Like in all aspects of life, too much of a good thing can be a bad thing. You just have to find balance.

* * * * *

I met Megan at the Highway House of Hope in January 2026 during a meaningful milestone—she was receiving her two-year recovery chip. When asked to share her journey, Megan gave a powerful personal testimony that resonated with everyone present. Afterward, I asked if she'd be willing to put her story in writing, and she graciously agreed. What follows is Megan's perspective on how AA helped save her life.

Megan M. Addiction and Recovery Story

Growing up, I had all a child could want. I grew up in an upper-middle-class family with my mom, dad, and younger brother. Everything I did came easy to me, and these things included playing tennis, softball, piano, competitive horseback riding, and always being at the top of my class in school. I had friends and went to church. I did all the things that a well-adjusted child growing up in a small town would do. My brother was a year and a half younger than me and was responsible for any and all of the drama or chaos that happened at home. By the time he was in middle school, he had been diagnosed with bipolar disorder and a list of other possible mental health disorders. He was in and out of treatment centers for depression and suicidal thoughts or attempts, and by the time he was in his late teens, he was diagnosed with schizophrenia. I took this on by deciding that I needed to be the child to make my parents proud. I couldn't create any waves. I had to be the easy one, the one that stuffed the uncomfortable emotions down and didn't cause them any worry. I needed to be perfect and make a success of myself.

Despite what I thought was a fairly idyllic life, I lived with the feeling that I couldn't be true to myself. I lived to make others happy and proud of me. I was insecure, afraid to share my opinions and feelings, and never completely comfortable in my own skin. I was reserved, stoic, shy, and unsure of my own voice. I began to hang out with a crowd in high school that introduced me to alcohol and drugs. It started with alcohol and pot, and I wasn't above drinking a couple bottles of Robitussin in one sitting either. I loved the feeling of escaping reality, and it didn't matter what the substance looked like. I finally felt like I could speak freely to others, and I didn't have to be perfect when I was intoxicated. I was partying every weekend, going to school under the influence, and began getting into trouble for truancy as I skipped classes to drink and get high. Through it all, I kept my grades up and graduated high school early so as not to alarm my parents too much. I moved away to go to college, where I got into drugs like cocaine, ecstasy, mushrooms, and acid, along with alcohol. I abused Adderall and prescription painkillers, which I justified by saying that they were the only way I could make it through school. I told myself I was managing my life well, but it would take me ten years to finally graduate college as a daily drug addict.

By the time I was twenty-one years old, I had a daily cocaine, alcohol, and Xanax habit. At this time I was introduced to heroin. Sitting in a car in my parents' driveway, the night before Thanksgiving, I tried heroin for the first time. I was so sick the next day that I spent Thanksgiving sprawled out on my parents' living room floor with them wondering if I needed to go to the emergency room. They had no idea that my "illness" was drug-induced, and, being the master manipulator that I was, I led them to believe I had just come down with something and I would be okay after I got some rest. Over the next year I became a daily heroin user and traded the cocaine in for methamphetamine. This would be the combination of drugs I needed to wake up with every morning for the next seventeen years.

The only periods of short sobriety I had over these years were those when I was locked up behind bars, pregnant, or institutionalized during the four times I went into treatment. With all the consequences that I had as a result of my addiction, I only thought I needed to learn to be a better drug addict. I needed to lie more, to be better at living a double life so "normal" people wouldn't know what I was really about. I lost my brother to suicide when I was twenty-five, and this only reinforced the idea in my head that I must be the one to make my parents proud. If I admitted I was an addict, that I needed help, wouldn't this only mean I was a loser and had failed at life? After all, I had wonderful parents who had only proved to me again and again how much they loved and cared for me. I couldn't let them down. It was this pride and unwillingness to admit the truth—that I'm an alcoholic and an addict with a disease—that I would eventually have to accept in order to find the path toward living a reasonably happy life in recovery.

During my active addiction I got married, had two children, and made it my goal to stay under the influence at all times while living a secret double life. I dressed my children up in the best clothes and sent them to private schools and to church with their grandparents every Sunday. All the while, I was spending my days and nights high on heroin and meth, doing everything I could to keep people from knowing who I really was. I had been arrested for various misdemeanors over the years, always with a slap on the wrist. In 2021, I got my first felony when I was arrested for possession of heroin. I was put on probation, and, despite the drug tests, the community service, and the classes I was required to take, it never crossed my mind that putting down the drugs was an option. In my mind, again, I just needed to be a better drug addict. I needed to be a better liar and figure out ways to outsmart all of the people that I thought were against me, especially law enforcement. I would sit in my bathroom for hours getting high while the kids were at school or asleep at night and talk to my husband and "using friends" about how I am not prison material. At the same time, I was doing everything that would send me straight to prison. I no longer knew how to live with the alcohol and drugs or how to live without them.

I had given up on all of my dreams, had lost any confidence I had in my abilities to achieve anything of substance in my life, and had almost nothing left to be proud of. If you asked me what I was proud of at that time, the only thing I could come up with and say with sincerity was that I was proud of being a mother and of how much I loved my children. I was using every day, never sleeping at night because I couldn't put the drugs down long enough to crawl into bed, but still doing my best to do all of the things I thought a loving mother should do. This all came crashing down when I was called into my son's school and the administration slid my mugshot in front of my face and asked me to explain. I was humiliated, ashamed, and left the school in tears as they asked me not to come on campus anymore. I could no longer show up to have lunch with my child, no longer volunteer as a parent at school, and no longer drive him to school or pick him up each day. Honestly, I shouldn't have been driving anyone anywhere at that time, but that's the insanity and denial of addiction. I thought I was still in control and had it together enough to do the things that life requires of us each day.

It was only a matter of weeks after I was banned from the school that I found myself in jail, with my probation revoked, after being arrested for theft when I acted on the brilliant idea to shoplift on Christmas Eve. All that talk of me not being prison material meant nothing now as I was transported off to prison with a two-year sentence. I served eleven months before I was released on parole. When I returned home and my children wrapped their arms around me, finally able to breathe again knowing that their mom was home, the only thing I was sure of was that I could never leave them like that again. A week later I relapsed. I figured eleven months was enough time for me to get my head on straight, get healthy again, and now I could dabble in drugs and control it. This relapse taught me that when I put one drink or drug in my body, I have no choice or control over how much more I use. From that first use, the mental obsession came on full force, and I was right back where I left off before I went away to prison. I became shady, started lying, lost the light in my eyes, and knew for the first time that if I didn't do something different, I was going back to prison or I was going to die.

The last day I put any mind-altering substances into my body was on January 23, 2024. I was miserable and had no idea how to live life sober. I was lonely, insecure, and more uncomfortable in my own skin than ever. This is when I walked into the doors of Alcoholics

Anonymous. I knew I had to put down the alcohol and drugs since I had been exposed to AA in the past while in rehab. Even so, I thought I was smarter than everyone else in the room and felt a certain pride in doing things my way without help. I began attending AA meetings almost every day, thinking the people seemed nice enough, and I couldn't help but see that the alcoholics in those rooms were just like me. I looked forward to going to meetings because it was the only time in my day where I felt a little bit of peace and comfort. I began to see that these were my people, and for the first time since I could remember, felt like I fit in without having alcohol or drugs on board. Still, I didn't think I needed to work the twelve steps, didn't think I needed a sponsor to help me, and wasn't sure that I was ready to make friends with anyone I met in those rooms. In truth, I didn't know how to have authentic relationships with others, and the idea of being honest and real with another person intimidated me.

"Keep coming back" is what they told me, so I did. As I sat in meetings and listened, I looked around and noticed the peace and contentment with life that my fellow alcoholics had. Life didn't seem as difficult for them as it felt for me. I was exhausted and wanted to know how they woke up happy and didn't have to fake a smile with everyone they came into contact with each day. I began to believe that a Higher Power could restore me to sanity, and if I was going to give my life over to the care of God, that meant working the steps. If I was going to work the steps, I decided I would have to get a sponsor to hold me accountable. I began accepting invitations to lunch after meetings and spending time with other alcoholics in recovery. People in AA accepted me for who I was. I remembered what it felt like to truly laugh, feel real joy, and slowly became secure in who I am. I met regularly with my sponsor as we worked the steps together, and this relationship would teach me how to be honest, let go of shame, and own my actions. I learned what humility looks like and that not having the answers to solve all of my life problems did not make me a failure. I was an alcoholic and needed the help of other alcoholics to learn to live a life of serenity, a life in recovery. I reconnected with the Higher Power I knew as a child, this time on a personal level, and understood that if I just do the next right thing, God will take care of the outcome.

At two years sober, all of the ninth-step promises have come true in my life. I'm humbled and in awe of the grace that God has shown me when I look at my life today. The obsession to drink or use that I thought I would have forever left as soon as I made the decision to surrender myself fully to the AA program. I have gone through divorce, death of a loved one, and many other difficult things in sobriety and can honestly say that the thought of taking a drink or using drugs never crossed my mind during any of it. The fellowship of

AA has been a gift that I never expected to come along with a life in recovery. I attend meetings regularly and love to sit in those rooms and know that my best friends are there with me. I talk to another alcoholic every day and do my best to keep my side of the street clean. I do service work by going into the jail and bringing AA meetings to the women who remind me so much of myself. I work with women who are on probation by volunteering to facilitate a program that teaches them how to see themselves for the women that God created them to be, and I get to use my experience, strength, and hope to plant seeds in their life. I know that my voice matters. I am welcome back on my child's school campus, even elevated to a position of trust as I now work at a school. I am no longer held back by the fear that others will judge me for the person I once was. I have purpose, show up for others, and am humbled and honored that today I get to show others the grace and love that was freely given to me by God and other alcoholics in recovery.

ELEVEN

Trusting Doctors and Therapists

Two of my heroes have been my psychiatrist and therapist. I'm not going to name them in this book, but both have had a critical role in my recovery: my psychiatrist is the gateway to my medications. Meds are critical, and they have to become a habit, but you also have to be certain you're taking the *right* medications. The right meds kept me alive in crucial spots in the past, and I know that they continue to keep me alive today. Once I accepted that, things started becoming more manageable.

My psychiatrist has probably saved my life three or four times, literally, since I've been with him. I call him one of my angels. He's been there any time I've needed him.

Med management is critical. When I was first diagnosed with bipolar disorder, my doctor asked me to do this little exercise. I wore glasses at the time, and he said,

"Paul, take your glasses off and read this sign behind my back." I looked at him a little funny, but said, "Okay. I'll do that." Then I realized—and told him plainly—"I can't read it." He said, "Okay, now put your glasses back on and try to read it." I did, and I could.

It's simple, but so important. He said to me, "Paul, medication is exactly like wearing glasses. If you don't wear your glasses, you can't see straight. And if you don't take your meds, you can't think straight. It's really no different than wearing your glasses, or contacts, to see. You just have to take them every day, starting with when you brush your teeth. It's a part of your life now, and it has to be. It's a new life now."

In the very beginning of my diagnosis, I didn't want to take the prescribed meds. Even though I'd been in psych care, and had had episodes of mental health, and manic episodes, hyper-manic episodes, and depressed episodes, I didn't want to think I needed them. I wanted to deny it. I wanted to believe it was just society's way of numbing people, but time has shown me I just cannot be without it. It's one of the most important things to staying alive.

Right off, it's also important to see that it will take time for the meds to begin to get into and work through your system. You might not feel much at first, even for a couple of weeks. It might take a few weeks or longer, but the effect does begin to take root. This is crucial; it's a psychiatric medication.

I went off the medication on my own, sometime around 2007-2008, for a number of weeks, and had another psychotic episode right before Kristen and I got married. That wasn't good. The attitude can easily become, "Ah, I don't need this stuff." Then I had another episode. That's where people can begin to abuse alcohol or drugs (or, re-abuse them), because they think those things can work instead of the medications prescribed to them.

My therapist is critical to my needs, but he realizes he's not there to prescribe, or control in any way, the meds. He says, "The behavioral health therapy is between you and I." He stays in his lane, in other words. It will be crucial for most people, their situations, needing this kind of help, to see these two roles as different. My therapist will ask whether I am taking my medication as prescribed; he'll just get that basic information. But he doesn't go further.

My therapist will tell me, "The rest of it is up to you, to do the work." Exercise, dieting, good sleeping habits, those things. The basic life skills become very important. But I've crossed any bridge where it's a temptation to come off the meds; no, I don't struggle with that temptation any more. I strongly encourage people to see that you simply have to accept this.

I did have one stretch where I was on the wrong medication. It just wasn't the best thing to be prescribed, but we didn't know that at the time. I was on it for two weeks and just kept getting worse. I ended up in the hospital. This kind of thing can happen. By no one's bad intention, you can find yourself on the wrong medication. I hadn't had acute mania in years, and there were many patients that this medication worked for without the side effects that the other meds had, so my doctor thought it was best to suggest it. You can have allergic reactions. Read yourself carefully, day to day, and have great discussions with your psychiatrist and therapist. Remember, they are there to help you.

I have the right medications for me today, and if there is an emergency, I know what to take. It's important to be at this place.

Why is a psychiatrist and/or therapist critical? I had an episode once where I was suicidal. My psychiatrist was the only person I wanted to talk with. It's a blur to this day; I can't remember the exact words said. But I do recall being at this point. I remember I walked into his office and he—and his office—cleared his entire schedule for like two hours just to meet with me. That's what a relationship can do, what it can mean. He did this just to get me back in the right state of mind. Needless to say, being suicidal is not a good place to be. He worked to get me back on track—and it took some time. But just being in his presence, him listening to me, it was lifesaving.

Also, you have to be patient with your psychiatrist. Not every doctor is going to get it right every time, all the time. People will respond differently to different prescribed drugs. The dose might be off—maybe too much, maybe not enough—and it has to be adjusted. One might have side effects that have too much of a detrimental effect. It's just a matter of getting the right balance for your body type and place in life. It takes time, and that is not easy. Believe me, patience is something I work on one day at a time as well!

Since my manic episode of 2021 my psychiatrist has recommended that I always review my Wellness Recovery Action Plan (otherwise known as WRAP). My psychiatrist has recommended I have one to prevent future relapses of mania. One of the main functions of a WRAP is to recognize when you're in a normal state of mind. For me, the top three things that indicate I'm trending toward an upward spiral of mania are a lack of sleep, feeling agitated, and my wife letting me know I need to take one of two medications that tranquilize a person to sleep more than you typically would.

Let me say just a little more about a WRAP. A Wellness Recovery Action Plan is a simple and powerful process for creating the life and wellness you want. With a WRAP, a person can:

- Discover simple, safe, and effective tools to create and maintain wellness

- Develop a daily plan to stay on track with your life and wellness goals

- Identify what throws you off track and develop a plan to keep moving forward

- Gain support and stay in control, even in a crisis

For those struggling with manic episodes, I wholeheartedly recommend talking with your doctor to develop a WRAP. This is one of the goals of this book: to give the right advice and tools to those with addictions and disorders. A WRAP is something that is critical for me.

The WRAP process supports you in identifying the tools that keep you well, and it helps create action plans to put them into practice in everyday life. Along the way, a WRAP helps you incorporate key recovery concepts and wellness tools into your plans and life.

The following information is from Mary Ellen Copeland, PhD, who developed WRAP in 1997 with a group of people who had lived through experiences of serious mental health challenges.

The key concepts of a WRAP:

- **Hope**. This brings out the belief that we can get well, stay well, and go on to fulfill our dreams and goals. This will also help us consider ways to increase hope in our own lives.

- **Personal responsibility.** It's up to each of us to take action and do what needs to be done to stay well. We get to decide what personal responsibility means to us and the steps we want to take to be responsible for ourselves and our wellness.

- **Education**. Learning all we can about what we are experiencing helps us make good decisions about all aspects of our lives. We can define education for ourselves and explore steps to learn more in any area.

- **Self-advocacy**. Reaching out to others and expressing our needs helps us get what we need, deserve, and want in support of our wellness and recovery. We can determine for ourselves how we want to self-advocate in different areas of our lives, including how we want to communicate our needs and preferences to others.

- **Support**. Receiving support from others, and giving support, will help us feel better and enhance our quality of life. We get to decide what support means to us, what we look for in supporters, and how we want to provide support as well as how we want to receive it.

The foundation of WRAP's six main parts form the wellness toolbox. These tools are used to build our WRAP. These form a list of skills and strategies for keeping ourselves well and feeling better if we don't feel well. Wellness tools are simple, safe, accessible, and often cost-free things we can do to recover or maintain our wellness. They give us hope and help us feel and stay connected to others and to ourselves.

Much more about this can be learned by visiting Human Potential Press and studying the work of Mary Ellen Copeland.

One of the biggest conclusions and truths that shape my days is that I have to look at life as staying balanced mentally, emotionally, physically, spiritually. My licensed therapist has a critical role. I like to call it "a check-up from the neck up." We go over how it's going in my relationships with my wife, my children, my parents, professionally, financially, socially, all these types of "buckets" that we navigate. I look at it a bit like a road map: past, present, and future moments.

What am I doing about these moments? Am I journaling, exercising, dieting, writing? My therapist calls them four quadrants we have to focus on: *physical, mental, spiritual, emotional.* Those aren't listed in any particular order; the key is to find balance with all of them. You can draw a circle or square or rectangle and box off four quadrants. Those areas have been critical for my therapist and I to talk about. Like four tires on a car: they all have to be reasonably balanced and full of air, right? I'll talk a bit more about the four, but keep that in mind for now: how critical each of the four are.

He also calls it "managing your 168"—managing those 168 hours we all have in one week. Everybody has the same amount of time. With my therapist, we call it "taking inventory" of your life. He likes to call it, "What is the rose of the week? What is the onion?" You know: what are the highs, or what are the lows, of last week? He might also ask: what are your three "feeling" words? "What are you feeling right now?" I think it's important to find three words that say a ton about how you are doing *right now.*

With that said, here are a few tools I have found useful that allow me to maintain my well-being mentally, physically, spiritually, and emotionally.

Exercise: Let me park on exercise for a couple of paragraphs: I've had an up and down time with that—probably like most people! There was a period when I was in the gym four to five times a week, an hour at a time. Very helpful. Then, the summer of 2024 it kind of got away from me for different reasons, then we moved the summer of 2025. That seems like a lot of different excuses, doesn't it? Again, I know many, even most, people fight the exercise self-will battle. Life happens, and I got out of the routine. I am always working to get back to a healthy routine in this area, but I have a tendency to ruminate and smoke my cigarettes during down time. My current therapist, psychologist, myself, and my wife are all hands on deck trying to help me get out of my own way.

I get frustrated with myself if I only have four days of exercise of one hour: four hours a week, in my mind, doesn't seem like much. Not enough, at least, for me.

But I need to be kinder to myself; that's not bad if I get four solid hours of exercise a week. And I know it's very important to me.

Journaling: Journaling is the best thing of all the disciplines for me. Right now, I am working on getting myself doing this instead of lighting a cigarette or picking up the phone or running an errand or looking on my phone. I have to start making it a non-negotiable in my morning routine. It's literally taking inventory of these sorts of things: how do I feel today? What am I grateful for? What are my emotions? Simple things are so important. I go through three things to be grateful for, three emotions I strongly feel about, and, how did I sleep last night? One to 10: what do I feel like? How do I feel today?

This only takes ten minutes a day, maybe fifteen, tops. But it does so much. If you don't journal, I highly recommend it.

Dieting: Here is another helpful area. When I'm aware of what I'm eating, I feel better. Maybe helping with meal prepping. My wife does the meal preparation part, while I handle the eating part. I do help with grocery shopping, but I could help more in the prep.

Sleep hygiene: This too is critical. Seven to eight hours of sleep per day is critical. I take this as seriously as I do my medications; sleep hygiene is critical. You have to manage your sleep. I'm pretty disciplined about this and am like a 10:30 PM–5:30 AM kind of sleeper.

I have a tendency to let poker and sports games try to take precedence in my mind, but I know that about myself. I have to remind myself of this when I want to invite friends over to watch a late game.

In short: there's a lot of work needed in staying healthy! You have to realize it's going to take a lot of work. Go back to the four quadrants. My therapist at times might draw out four quadrants in a circle, or just talk about them. But he might park on exercise. What are you doing there? You can make walking the dog part of your exercise quadrant, because it is! You can swim, lift weights, whatever.

Within those four quadrants, focusing on critical things is the key. Here are some of those things.

He might ask me: what are you doing spiritually for yourself? Are you reading certain material? Are you praying, meditating?

The emotional part: same, so we talk about journaling. Learning to pause when agitated, or maybe doubtful, about life. How are you managing your emotions?

Then mentally: we might discuss the medications regimen, my sleep hygiene.

Physically: are you going to the gym, do you have a leash to walk your dog, ride a bicycle, walk with your wife, swim, move your body for 20 minutes?

We might dive deeper into any of these quadrants at any one particular meeting.

So it's a question of looking at balance and being aware. It will help me see if I'm weak in this area or that area. I might not be exercising enough as I've said, so the quadrants help me see that that tire is out of balance. Again, think like a car or truck. If you were going to go on a road trip, you'd check everything first: oil, gas, tires, fluids. Well, what's the check-up on your life? To get through certain challenging seasons in life, you have to make sure you are physically, mentally, spiritually, and emotionally fit. Again, not necessarily in that, or any, order. I need check-ups even for things like moving to Texas, or just being a parent. Real challenges in life.

One of the biggest reasons Kristen and I talked ourselves out of moving to Texas in the past is the fact that we would have to leave our therapy team. We are now here in Texas and have found some really cool new team members. I have a therapist that is still growing on me, but I still check in with my old therapist from time to time. I have a new psychiatrist who I really respect and am enjoying getting to know. It also helps that she is getting me set up with a primary care physician. That is something I have not allowed myself to do in the past. I tend to get myself into self-sabotage from time to time, but I am working on it. Kristen and I found a new couples' therapist, and we have recently started attending family sessions with our three daughters. Our goal now is to show our daughters how helpful talk therapy is for a healthy life.

* * * * *

Kristen and my dad are invaluable as well. I'm blessed to have both my parents alive. I wrote about Kristen earlier in the book. My dad and I will do all sorts of things together—we love going to sporting events—but one of the most valuable things he'll do is get me out on the golf course, which is what I love.

You can put this under the exercise category, the physical quadrant. Golf is great exercise in that you are constantly walking with or without a riding cart, using different muscle groups, and working on hand-eye coordination.

I wrote about golf earlier, I know, but I want to say again that golf is something, for me, like therapy, and I can use it to check off a bit of the exercise box on my to-do list. I love being outside and enjoying the game, and I can just zone out and cancel out everything else in life. I can get time with my dad or a friend and—I don't mean to be light about this comment—I don't care about anything else until my next shot. Golf is a one-shot-at-a-time kind of game.

It's a game, but it's exercise, and it's therapeutic. Find your game of golf in life.

TWELVE

Family, Heroes, and Moving Forward in Life

When it comes to talking about heroes, nobody outranks my wife, three daughters, parents, and immediate family. My therapists are in that mix also. I wrote about them at the end of the previous chapter. They are a big reason I can move forward. I know I put in the work, I take action, but the one thing I know about myself is feedback is important for me in taking the steps that I do. No one can do it for me, but I respond to how others react to me. Sometimes this is to my own detriment, but I really care what others think.

But first, I want to provide some context to my professional life. Today I manage a commercial building in Corrales, New Mexico. I manage a total of 19 rental units within the building—management, standard maintenance, and repairs. It requires a lot to keep up with.

But like those rental units, life is all about maintenance, care, and upkeep of yourself. There is much I work on with my past, present, and future. It's a total life balance—and this is a word you hear a lot, right? "Work-life balance." But instead of that word, I like the word *harmony*. Life is somewhat like a symphony, where every piece has to play together and complement each other nicely.

So I go back to where I've come from: recovery. I remind myself of this simple phrase: "There is no graduation." There is always a place of striving to move forward, of reaching for excellence in your inner self, even though you're rarely going to have it.

I've thought about coaching others, not only mentally but professionally. I do a lot of professional service with all I've done with the funeral and cemetery business, pet business, and now my property management business. I'd like to see where God takes me regarding coaching and helping others.

Much earlier in the book, I wrote about my parents, how they have inspired me. I had my editor sit down and talk with my parents to help provide their perspective. I'll intermix some of my thoughts through this next section, but I think it helps to show where I came from. Their roots are my roots, their story is my story. For good or bad, they shaped who I am.

Leonor is my mom and Kevin is my father. I have heard so much about generational trauma, but my parents worked so hard to give me the best childhood despite the trauma they endured. They did that for me, and I am striving to do that for my girls.

* * * * *

Leonor: I was 18 when I came to the States. I was going through a lot. I had lost my mom a couple of years before. It left you so busy with life, busy with just trying to survive. At that time, my little sister was in a coma. My brother Henry and I came to the States. My little sister died two to three months after I got married. I don't remember a lot of feeling about that then. I think later in life is when those emotions hit me.

Kevin and I dated two years before we married. As Paul said, we met in the small restaurant where I worked; Kevin was a young police officer. Then when we began to live life, and we made the choice to move to Delaware, when Kevin left the state police and went back into the funeral business, that's when the next big changes in life hit me. Your siblings are back in New Mexico. You've moved from Mexico to New Mexico to now Delaware on the east coast of the United States. You miss the close ties you have with your family, your food, all that.

Kevin: We moved primarily for financial reasons. As a state policeman, you made very little money. My father died in a road accident—turns out, that was the same week that Leonor's little sister died. While I was at my dad's funeral, I was offered a job to come back to Delaware [in the funeral and cemetery business].

That was a lot of stress. Lenor had recently lost her mom and a sibling. I had lost my father and a sibling also. But we matched well: although we came from different backgrounds and cultures, those backgrounds and cultures were also very similar in a number of ways.

My father [Paul's grandfather] instilled an incredible work ethic in all of his children. My dad had me and my siblings working since turning 13 years old. For my jobs, I traveled a lot, had a lot of stress. When I decided to start my businesses here in New Mexico, Paul was just starting college. I would work 16-18 hours a day, up to seven days a week. I moved here by myself, the family back in Texas, and had big loans. "How am I going to pay these back?" That sort of thing. But I was determined to work my way through it.

Paul: These sorts of things inspired me, helped me see that life takes a lot of hard work. My parents helped me so much when I went through very dark periods. They still inspire me today.

Leonor: I'm involved with NAMI (the National Alliance on Mental Illness). I go every week. Every time I'm in a meeting on Tuesday afternoons, honestly, I feel like I am the luckiest person. I owe that to Paul. He has done everything to stay healthy. He's what you call very "recovery compliant."

When I talk to people in the meetings, it's due to Paul that I can help them. I give them hope. They will say: "Oh my God, I now have hope." At those meetings, you will see families, moms, in the worst possible pain, unsure how to help their children. Then, people who have come through the other side can really help. They say, "Thank you so much."

When Paul was in the hospital, I think I had PTSD over that. We were with Paul four to five days and nights to get him out of the hospital. Then one morning, you hear: "Get up, Paul's in jail." I was scared. How could that happen?

We were very confused, very hurt. But you realize that the system failed Paul, it failed us. So at a [NAMI] meeting, I can feel the pain of those parents. When Paul was in that hospital, they put him in jail instead of helping him.

I also learn—every time I go to a meeting, I learn. It can be sad to be there. Very sad. But you work to give hope. The majority of the kids, the people, who have the illness, don't do what Paul has done, haven't put in the work Paul has. They don't. And yet, a lot of them are also harmless.

I always thank Paul—for giving us a good life.

Kevin [on Paul's hospital stay that ended with him in jail]: You go to a staff to get help. You think they are professional, there to help you, but too many of them are very incompetent . . . and you end up in jail. And the same sorts of things, of attitudes, can be true with the people running the jail. I spent up to 24 hours a day meeting with attorneys, lawyers, police officers—working hard to get him out of jail and into UNM [University of New Mexico Hospital, which has a mental health wing]. The people in that hospital acknowledged that what happened to Paul in the first hospital should not have happened.

If we, if the right people, hadn't been there to help get Paul out of jail, who knows what could have happened?

Leonor: Kristen spent hours telling the hospital staff that they were supposed to help Paul calm down and go to sleep, but the reaction to the meds he was given was the opposite. It's called a paradoxical reaction.

Leonor [on Paul being in Cottonwood Recovery]: Paul wanted to go there. He wanted to do it. We couldn't do it for him. We were there for his family, for Kristen. We took the girls. We all learned a lot from each other during that period.

Kevin: It was a good experience for Paul, that facility and program. It was excellent for Paul, the right place at the right time. I knew from past experience and family that Paul needed to be in a facility, the right facility.

There was family counseling. We went for a two-day session. Sometimes Paul was involved in that meeting, sometimes just family counselors were involved. They did very thorough family meetings.

Leonor [looking back to UNM, the second hospital, after jail]: At UNM, they got Paul to be more stable, and then we were able to bring him home.

Kevin: There were legal issues that followed. We had to go in front of a judge. There was a long list of stipulations. I had to sign to be personally responsible for a year, or until the judge released him from that. Paul had to check in regularly. He had to go to a county-run program for a year. He had to report in, get documents signed, and then report back to the judge.

Paul: I had two felony counts for battery against a health care worker [for what happened in the first hospital]. That was why I faced such strict consequences in front of the judge. I had to stay with my parents, and I couldn't leave for a month. So I couldn't see my wife and three girls. All put together, that was about two months where I didn't get to see my own family. The girls were 11, 9, and 6.

Kevin: He's a lucky guy, is all I can say. Kristen went through a lot of stress. We were there with her, praying, crying. We had to plead with the judge to allow him to go into that [second] hospital.

Leonor: Kristen and I were hugging and jumping up and down when the judge said he could go to [UNM] hospital.

Kevin: We just encourage Paul. I've been involved in a 12-step program since I was a teenager. I always remind Paul to take care of his recovery, that it will never stop. Both alcohol and bipolar, neither of those will ever entirely go away. They have different recovery and different treatment needs. We're fortunate that Paul has been very compliant on all fronts. He knows we're always there for him.

Paul: I say that it is a dual diagnosis, and it takes a dual recovery.

Leonor [when Paul's family moved from New Mexico to Texas in early 2025]: His move was hard on us. It was really the first time Paul was not [physically] close to us. It's a 12-to-13-hour drive [to their Texas home] from Albuquerque. But we're lucky that we're still young enough that we can do it. Eventually, when we can't drive, we will move closer to him.

* * * * *

Hail Cesar

In the early days of my diagnosis, with my parents, there were a lot of tears. They didn't have a way of knowing what was wrong with me. Cesar, though, had a way of making things easier for me. I think it was because he didn't change who he was around me. He was just himself, and that was just what I needed.

When I was first diagnosed Cesar went out of his way to move from Santa Fe, New Mexico to Albuquerque to hang out with me and make sure I was okay. He made a huge sacrifice for my life moving to be closer to me in

2004. For that I am forever grateful for his endless love and support.

We would play chess, Monopoly, and just hang out and watch the *Sopranos* when I was first diagnosed.

My cousin Cesar: he's like a brother to me, a big brother; he's early 50s, so he's nine years older than me. He's the cousin who was at the hospital with my aunt Connie when I was born (I did not have an actual brother.) Cesar (pronounced *SE-sar*), what does he mean to me? If I have some problems, he just shows up at my house. Literally. No questions asked. He used to be just two hours away, but now it's 13 to 14 hours, so that's a bit of distance now. He's in New Mexico, but comes for work out here in Texas and has already visited twice. We haven't lived here a year yet! I speak with Cesar four to five times a week, even if just like three to five minutes each. We call each other all the time.

I call Cesar a "no questions asked" friend. If I'm having a bad day, he is there. And again, he has literally just shown up at my house. If I've had a bad episode, he just shows up. He's the type of friend who can help make things right again. If one of us can't catch the phone at the time of a call, we always call back, within a few hours, as soon as reasonably possible.

He is one of my heroes in my life, so I wanted to make sure I had a space about him in this book. Thank you, primo.

* * * * *

Kristen's parents and family

I'd like to devote some of my words to Kristen's family and parents who have supported us so much. We moved closer to them, just outside of San Antonio, Texas in May of 2025 after more than 23 years in New Mexico.

My parents were a big reason we were in New Mexico, and they started traveling so much more, as they should in retirement, so we were not seeing them as much for the last few years. I know they would be there for us in a heartbeat, but it seemed like it was silly to stay in New Mexico. After watching the crime get worse and worse and get really close to home, we decided it was time.

I wanted to be closer to Kristen's parents in Texas. Her sister just had her first baby, and not long after we decided to move, we found out she was pregnant again!

My in-laws are Carl and Brenda Olson. They have been married 43 years. They raised three kids, Kristen being the oldest. I first met Kristen's parents on a date night, at a Chili's, in the spring of 2002. Carl, an engineer, has been another anchor in my life, like a second father. He is a total family man. He worked 35 years for the same company, but is now retired.

Before I proposed to Kristen in Spain, I was attending an international conference for our funeral business in Las Vegas. Before I flew out to Las Vegas, I secretly flew out to Austin to ask him. I didn't tell Kristen where I was going or what I was doing, but I did tell my dad. He was very excited for me, and Carl was excited too.

After the wedding, Carl and I became even closer. I have so much respect for how he rose and took care of his family at such a young age. Carl's perspectives on life and family help me a lot. The way he and his wife care for each other has taught me so much. When I was incarcerated, Carl and Brenda dropped everything to come help. They never miss our kids' birthdays. Their love is unconditional.

I can see where my wife gets her kindness, willingness to help, and patience. Her mom and dad truly embody these things. Their love knows no bounds.

Every year for about 20 years, we all go to South Padre Island the first week of June with the whole family. We camp out on the beach and just hang out. We have the entire family—about 40 people, with aunts, uncles, cousins, friends and all that—and Carl spearheads all of this.

My dad loves Carl too. We all try to get together for golf outings as much as we can. The three of us have traveled to Mexico together, and I am so grateful for those memories.

These people became the heroes of my life. I often will tear up just thinking about them. Both sets of parents showed me unconditional love. No matter what happened, or happens, my family was, and is, always there. I have also been blessed by one friend from high school, a few from college, neighbors, and guys from AA who I consider brothers. Sometimes I get to points in my life where I feel like no one really cares, but I know this is not true. I am loved, and I love them in return.

I think I could write a whole book on all of the ways friends and family have shown up for me. Kristen reminds me that it is a true testament of how I make others feel when I am around them. She says so many people love me because I know how to pull people in and give them "a seat at our table," literally. This is also something that annoys Kristen at times as well! Friendships are not one-sided, and I like to show up for my friends. I guess that is why they show up for me.

I know many people are not as lucky as I am in this area. In realizing this fact, it made me want to help others less fortunate than me.

THIRTEEN

My Foundation, and Final Thoughts

As we come to the end of this book, I thought I'd leave the reader with some final thoughts. Although this book has taken more than three years to write, it's also taken a lifetime of experiences living with bipolar disorder and alcohol and drug addiction to come to formulate my conclusions.

Regardless of your gender, race, age, political views, or ethnicity, mental health is something we are all affected by. This book is designed to share my story of living with a mental illness in the hope of helping any person who comes in contact with this reality understand why mental health awareness is important for all walks of life. The stigma is counterproductive, and we can all do our part to help. Whether it is you or someone you love, what you do or don't do makes a difference. Take care of yourself, plug yourself into circles of influence that want to add to your life, and help someone else if you are able!

I'm *alive now* because I chose to practice recovery, and hopefully we can work together to save other children, adults, and families who live with someone with mental disorders and co-occurring disorders.

In my mind, having a dual diagnosis is no different than living with terminal cancer. You can choose to fight to not give up, or work a treatment plan that will allow you to live your best life one day at a time. Dual diagnosis may have been the cards you were given, but dual recovery is a choice. If you are not practicing recovery, your other choices are rehabilitation, incarceration/prison, a psychiatric hospital, or death.

So many quotes and sayings have stuck with me over the years that keep me going. I want to leave you with a few to hopefully inspire strength and hope through my experience so that you can change your life for the better one day at a time:

"Change is inevitable but growth is optional." "Learn from yesterday, live for today, hope for tomorrow."

My world seems to always be rapidly changing and taking me through ups and downs, but I am so grateful the human connection of living has always seen me through.

Sometimes the nicest thing you can do for yourself is to be nice to you. Give yourself grace. Rest and relax your mind, body, and spirit. We gave our daughters the middle names of Grace, Faith, and Hope, and I think that is a recipe for a life of recovery, don't you think?

During the process of writing this book I decided to create a nonprofit called the Alive Now Foundation. Our mission at Alive Now is to empower and educate children, adults, and families facing mental health challenges and addictions through collaborations with organizations doing big things. We hope that we can direct people to professionals offering personalized wellness programs that inspire hope, healing, and the pursuit of their best lives. Our foundation's goal is to save one life a day, 365 days a year. We will do that through grant writing and scholarships.

This book has also been incredibly therapeutic for me. In chapter 1 I discussed my experience with being in solitary confinement, naked in a jail cell. I made an agreement with myself: instead of filing a lawsuit against the hospital for medical malpractice, I decided to write my story, my way, in the hope of helping other people who live with mental health and addiction issues. I think I can do a lot more good with the latter. My hope is that my words, experiences, and life story can save other families heartache and even save lives.

* * * * *

Relapse and recovery have been part of my journey for more than twenty years of living with bipolar disorder and addiction. This is my story, and I'm grateful to be alive now to share it.

Our mission at the Alive Now Foundation is to empower individuals and families facing mental health challenges and addictions.

A person might ask me, "How can I help you support the mission and goal of the Alive Now Foundation?" My first response is you can volunteer your time to the organization and support our mission in some way. You can get involved in your local community to spread the word of what we're all about. You can sponsor a family member who lives with a mental illness or drug and alcohol addiction to enable them to get help. You can donate to the Alive Now Foundation and help spread the word of our goal of saving one life a day 365 days a year. You can also support us through buying a book for a family member or friend.

The Foundation has a board of directors which began business at the end of 2025/start of 2026, and we are getting to work on developing grants and scholarships, and raising awareness in the community. My thanks to individuals like Jade Bock with Building Beloved Communities for making the Foundation a reality. I'm forever grateful for your endless support at ANF.

We are the Alive Now Foundation, here to make a difference in the world. *You are alive now, and that is where we begin.*

For more information on how you can get
involved and access other resources,
please visit **www.alivenowfoundation.org**
or scan the QR code below.

A FINAL POEM

I love this poem. The author is unknown. I keep a copy of it around my work area.

I think it says so much. I'll close with this.

The Bottom Line

Face it: nobody owes you a living
What you achieve or fail to achieve in your lifetime
is directly related to what you do
Or fail to do
No one chooses his parents or childhood
But you can choose your own direction
Everyone has problems and obstacles to overcome
But that too is relative to each individual
NOTHING IS CARVED IN STONE
You can change anything in your life
if you want to badly enough
Excuses are for losers:
Those who take responsibility for their actions
Are the real winners in life
Winners fight life's challenges head on
Knowing there are no guarantees
And give it all they've got
And never think it's too late or too early to begin
Time plays no favorites
And will pass whether you act or not
TAKE CONTROL OF YOUR LIFE
Dare to dream and take risks
Compete . . .
If you aren't willing to work for your goals
Don't expect others to
BELIEVE IN YOURSELF
You're
ALIVE NOW so begin there.

HIGHWAY HOUSE OF HOPE
H
BOERNE, TX
KEEP
COMING BACK
IT WORKS IF
YOU WORK IT.
&
YOU ARE
WORTH IT!

www.ingramcontent.com/pod-product-compliance
Lightning Source LLC
Jackson TN
JSHW080924260226
98596JS00012B/70

9781968127312